Praise for *Bend the Healthcare Trend*

"An insightful and practical book that provides intelligent counsel on how to create, evaluate, and manage consumer-driven health plans and employee wellness programs. *Bend the Healthcare Trend* is an important contribution to lowering healthcare costs and promoting individual responsibility."

- Kevin Counihan, former CEO Healthcare.gov

"With a commitment to health and wellness, *Bend the Healthcare Trend* is right on target with a new approach to encouraging health and wellness with transparency, responsibility, and opportunity. Individuals become invested when they are empowered and engaged to take responsibility for their own health with education, initiatives, and resources. Mark and Jennifer's passion and commitment to providing solutions for the healthcare trend is exemplified in these written words."

—Deborah Hodges, President and CEO, Health Plans, Inc.

"By focusing on consumerism and well-being—two concepts often absent from the seemingly endless healthcare debates in America—*Bend the Healthcare Trend* offers some new and innovative twists on some very old problems —Robert Stone, Executive Vice President, Berkley Accident & Health*

"*Bend the Healthcare Trend* makes a clear case for the positive impact of greater cost transparency and consumer-driven engagement. This second edition brings fresh insights to the dialogue about health care in America."

—Claire Leheny, Executive Director, Association of Independent Schools in New England

"Must-read material for corporate leaders and human resource teams."

—Christopher Brown, President & CEO, Berkley Accident & Health

"As someone who deals with the constant dilemmas and drawbacks of our healthcare system, I found that *Bend the Healthcare Trend* provides employers and industry advisors a true vision of what drastic changes need to be made, how to implement the vision, and what breakthroughs we can achieve. An inspiring read."

—Adam Russo, CEO, The Phia Group, LLC

How Consumerism, Health & Well-being Transforms
Your Culture and Lowers Insurance Costs

Bend the
Healthcare Trend

MARK S. GAUNYA AND JENNIFER A. BORISLOW

STRATEGIC VISION PUBLISHING

The Health Dollar Equity Builder™, The Health Dollar Maximizer™, The Health Dollar Value Builder™ are trademarks of Strategic Vision Publishing, LLC. All rights reserved.

ISBN: 978-1-54390-249-5

SECOND EDITION
Strategic Vision Publishing, LLC
1 Griffin Brook Drive
Methuen, MA 01844

For more information on Mark S. Gaunya and/or Jennifer A. Borislow, email info@ strategicvisionpublishing.com

Copies of this book may be purchased for educational, business, or promotional use. Please contact orders@strategicvisionpublishing.com.

Printed in U.S.A.

This publication is not a substitute for the advice of your insurance advisor, accountant, lawyer, or any of your other advisors, personal or professional.

Neither the authors nor the publisher is rendering insurance, accounting, tax, or other professional services by publishing this book. As each individual's situation is unique, questions relevant to personal insurance needs should be addressed by an appropriate professional to ensure that the situation has been evaluated carefully and appropriately.

Neither the authors nor the publisher make any representations about the suitability of the information contained in this book, and all such information is provided "as is" without warranty of any kind. The authors and publisher specifically disclaim any liability, loss, or risk that is incurred as a consequence, directly or indirectly, of the use and/or application of any of the contents of this work.

Some case study names and details have been changed to protect the privacy of individuals mentioned.

To my wonderful wife, Debbie, and our three beautiful children,
Grayson, Kelly, and Brooke—you are my life.

Mark S. Gaunya

To my husband, Mike; our children, Jessica and Lauren;
and my parents, Wil and Margaret Kurth—I would not be the person
I am without your love, support, and encouragement.

Jennifer A. Borislow

TABLE OF CONTENTS

Foreword

Mark Gaunya and Jennifer Borislow have been representing the interests of small and midsize employers, and their employees and their families, using a variety of purchasing and plan design strategies for years. They are very creative and forward thinking.

For years, they have persuasively argued that the healthcare system would be more accountable and more effective if it was more transparent. There has been some progress on this issue, but much more remains to be done. Pioneer Institute in Massachusetts just published a report that indicated that many care providers could not answer basic cost questions for prospective patients about common, routine procedures.

Health plans have made efforts to make more cost and quality information available for their members as they make decisions about elective outpatient and inpatient procedures. In addition, state and federal government agencies have posted cost and quality information in various formats for certain procedures using a variety of rankings, rating systems, and publicly accessible websites.

Many would argue that this collection of initiatives is useful, but not as accessible or as comprehensive as they will need to be to truly change the dialogue between patients, care providers, and carriers.

As cost and quality data become more robust and easier to use, and as more and more people become more comfortable accessing it, it has the potential to help everyone improve quality and bend the healthcare trend.

Sophisticated advisors like Mark and Jennifer have been helping their clients use data to make better decisions for many years. Their decision to update the findings and ideas that made the first edition of this book so helpful to so many is a worthy effort.

Hopefully, it will encourage others to work on new tools and new ways of sharing useful clinical and cost information, so that the healthcare system can continue to become more transparent and more effective.

Charles D. Baker, Governor of Massachusetts

Acknowledgments

This is the second edition of *Bend the Healthcare Trend*; it builds on the original, published in 2009. Both books are almost forty years in the making—marking a journey that started in health care, traveled through corporate America in insurance, and continues through employee benefits brokerage and consulting. Somewhere in the midst of those collective experiences, I found my passion and a sense of purpose to make our healthcare system better for people by making it about them—helping them build their healthcare confidence.

As the son of Steve and Denise Gaunya (physical therapist and nurse), I was introduced to the entrepreneurial world of a healthcare provider. I watched them help many people and also struggle to build a sustainable business. They exposed me to the challenges of being an entrepreneur, and they provided me opportunities most young men in their early twenties do not enjoy—a seat at the table and the ability to participate in growing a business. I am forever grateful to my parents for instilling in me the values of hard work, a good education, and solid relationships with family and friends.

I worked for my parents for five years, helped them build, sell, and wind down their business and then went to work for two big health and welfare insurance companies in Washington, DC, and Chicago for the next six years. Then a pivot moment happened in my career when I accepted an executive sales leadership role with Destiny Health, a start-up consumer-driven health insurance company with a parent company based in South Africa, the birthplace of consumer-driven health care. As the sales leader, I worked with an amazing team and helped build an insurance company from the ground up that would fundamentally change the way people look at health insurance. (This was before HRAs and HSAs existed.) The value of that experience is hard to measure, and it's still paying dividends today through the creation of Captivated Health ®.

As Destiny Health grew, it expanded into other markets and formed new strategic partnerships. Destiny Health and Tufts Health Plan joined forces, and we relocated to Hopkinton, just outside of Boston. On our way, I met Jennifer Borislow—my business partner of the past twelve years and one of my closest friends. Together, we lead a thriving regional employee benefits and strategic advisory practice working with talented, world-class professionals and wonderful clients we enjoy helping. I will always be grateful to Jen for asking me to be her business partner; together we are 1 + 1 = 3 and that has translated into exponential growth for our business over the past decade.

Our entrepreneurial, innovative, bubbling company continues to disrupt the status quo. In July 2014, we launched a new division called Captivated Health ® —an innovative health and well-being financing solution for middle-market employers (50–500), which gives its member organizations control and information in a completely transparent environment and a unique "members first" personal experience supported by mobile technology and a concierge service for employees and families that makes health care about them rather than the system. Captivated Health ® is our exponential, national opportunity to make a difference in health care – to make it about the people.

A big part of our success is our *great* team members and the work they do for our clients. They are dedicated, passionate professionals on a mission with us to build a community of health and well-being one client at a time—and we are very grateful for their contribution and passionate dedication.

And finally, I have to say a word of gratitude to our clients. Thank you for your partnership and support over the years. Your stories are the proof that consumer-driven health and well-being plans lower insurance costs and change lives. We are grateful for your trust in us as your strategic advisor, and we are passionate about the work we do for you. We embrace our responsibility to look after you, your employees, and their families. It is our honor and privilege to serve you and make a difference.

There are many more people who have touched my life and career . . . too many to mention. To all of you who I didn't mention by name and who helped me along the way, thank you. Thank you for your friendship, guidance, support, and encouragement. I hope you enjoy this second edition!

Mark S. Gaunya

The first edition of *Bend the Healthcare Trend* was written eight years ago and was considered required classroom reading at three different universities. We wrote the book as a way to share our collective knowledge, expertise, and passion for consumer-driven health plans and building a culture of health and well-being. It is remarkable to see the changes in peoples' understanding and the growing acceptance of CDHP. We are grateful that our work has played an important role in helping people understand the value of being more engaged in their healthcare choices.

Fast-forward to today. So much has happened in the healthcare industry. The introduction of the Affordable Care Act (ACA), changes in our political system, industry regulation, advanced technology, and escalating pharmacy costs, just to name a few. The greatest challenge still remains affordability. We feel that the principles outlined in the book—transparency, responsibility, and opportunity—are timeless and, taken together, represent the cornerstone of what needs to happen to reduce the cost of health care. We remain passionately committed to educating and creating awareness about CDHP and creating a culture of health and well-being. We feel this book is a powerful tool to assist in that process.

There are a few people I want to acknowledge. First, my coauthor: Mark and I have been business partners and best friends for more than 12 years. I treasure our relationship and am grateful every day that he shares his talents, vision, and passion with me. The secret to our partnership is shared values, utmost respect, love, and an endless supply of creativity and innovation. We epitomize the phrase "Work hard, play hard, all day and every day," and we enjoy doing both at a high level.

At Borislow Insurance, we are blessed with an extremely talented group of individuals who allow us to focus on innovation and developing new client strategies. A very special acknowledgement and thank you goes to Pam Verrill and Dave Shore. Their leadership is remarkable and instrumental in helping us build an entrepreneurial and innovative company. Dave and Pam are masterful in helping us manage constant change. I must not forget Colleen Nagri, my right hand and the guardian of everything in my world. She was hugely instrumental in helping us get this revised edition completed.

Mark and I are grateful to these team members for their dedication, hard work, and commitment to continuously leading our organization and making a difference in the lives of our team members and our clients.

To our amazing clients, we are grateful for your partnership and the ability to work closely together. We are passionate about the work we do to help you save time and money and create a culture of health and well-being at your schools and companies.

And finally, with gratitude and appreciation, I also want to acknowledge the unconditional love and support of my husband Mike, our daughters, Jess and Lauren, and my many lifelong friends and business colleagues. My family and my close friendships are what I treasure the most. I remain incredibly blessed to be surrounded by such a special group of people.

Jennifer A. Borislow

Introduction

Albert Einstein is one of many purported to have said, "The definition of insanity is doing the same thing over and over again and expecting different results." Think about this quotation for a second, and ask yourself whether it applies to the way you manage your company's health insurance benefits.

Have you been doing the same thing over and over, expecting different results? If so, you will want to keep reading.

Double-digit increases in healthcare costs pose a growing challenge for all Americans. The United States spent around $3.35 trillion on health care in 2016, and that number is expected to rise to over $4.6 trillion by 2020. Healthcare costs made up 17.8% of our GDP in a recent year, and are currently growing at two to three times the rate of inflation.[1] All of this, of course, follows the passage of the Affordable Care Act in 2010—a measure that was supposed to bring healthcare costs down.

The escalating costs of health care and our growing reliance on health services continue to make both employers and employees nervous. If prices continue to rise, will Americans be able to afford access to healthcare services?

Roughly 56% of all Americans are covered by employer-provided health insurance, and 10.3% cover their own costs.[2]

Most employers can no longer afford to make purchasing decisions about the company health plan without engaging their employees. It's time for employers to ask employees to get engaged, change their behavior, and become more aware of their lifestyle choices and how they use—and pay—for healthcare services. This essential, long-overdue conversation is among the many things the Affordable Care Act, popularly known as Obamacare, has failed to support since its passage.

Employees must understand that they are consumers and that, as consumers, they have choices. Employers need to provide their employees with information that supports good choices, and the incentives to make positive, long-lasting changes that benefit both the employee and the employer.

Do you know the price of a smart TV, a pair of running shoes, or a car? You probably have an idea of the cost of each, and you wouldn't buy any of them without first doing some research and comparison shopping. Like most people, you'd want to find the best price for the highest quality product you could afford. Accordingly, you would shop around before deciding where to spend your money.

Comparison shopping is a normal part of consumer behavior. So why do we behave differently when evaluating and purchasing our healthcare options?

Do you know the cost of an emergency room visit, the cost of choosing a brand-name drug over a generic alternative, or the cost of a night in a hospital? If you don't, odds are your employees don't either. And if consumers don't know the costs, they can't possibly make informed decisions about their purchases.

Most consumers don't use the same discretion when purchasing health insurance or healthcare services as they do when purchasing a new car. Although choosing a new car is a big decision, making informed choices about which health insurance plan to select and how to take the best care of your health is far more important ... and in many cases costs as much as or more than a good used car on an annual basis!

Supporting the Consumer's Right to Choose

Let's consider the car analogy a little more closely. Just because you're familiar with Ford vehicles doesn't mean you're going to buy one. There are many makes and models of cars, so you'll likely do research on the Internet, check the Blue Book value, and visit different dealerships to see who's offering the best cars for the best prices. Based on your needs, you'll choose the type of vehicle that suits you. If you're a member of a five-person family, you might consider a minivan. If you're single, a compact two-seater might be more your style. You'll also choose from the manufacturer's list of available options to customize your new car. If you live in an area that gets a lot of snow, you'll probably want a four-wheel-drive vehicle. If you have young children, you might want a DVD player in the backseat.

Insurance plans, like vehicles, are made up of different options, so why wouldn't you want to choose one that addresses your group's specific health and budget concerns? If consumers of automobiles bought only what was traditional or the first product on the market, we'd all still be driving Model Ts! We're not, though, and that's because carmakers understand that consumers want options. In the same way, we believe insurance plans can and should support the consumer's right to choose. And that's why we wrote this book.

Consumers should be free to make purchasing decisions about health care that speak to their values, that don't support arbitrary and unnecessary cost increases, that give them more control over their spending, and that require the acceptance of a certain level of personal responsibility for their own health and well-being. That point of view may not be popular among government bureaucrats, or among healthcare providers and insurers who have grown used to a world in which cost transparency is all too often rare or nonexistent. It is, however, a point of view that we believe employers must adopt if they wish to do right by their employees, and to survive and thrive in an era of unrestrained cost increases.

So, for example, if your employees want to seek care at large teaching hospitals, they need to understand that they may pay a little more for that care. They must decide for themselves whether the higher cost justifies the value. In Massachusetts, for example, the cost of seeking care at many teaching hospitals is approximately 30% higher than at a community hospital—yet the care isn't necessarily worth 30% more. Consumers have different needs, but the one thing they all agree on is the desire to have choice when it comes to accessing healthcare providers and services.

The challenge is that employees don't appreciate the full value of their health insurance plans and the cost that their employers incur to provide that benefit. Employees want choices ... but they don't necessarily want to pay for them, and their first instinct is often to make snap decisions in areas where they haven't been given enough information. The average American employee who needs family insurance spends just a few minutes each year during open enrollment making a health insurance buying decision—surely a major purchase if there ever was one. This is a failure of the system, and addressing that failure is one of the major aims of *Bend the Healthcare Trend*.

How Did We Get Here?

If health care is already costing the United States so much money, how is it possible that costs continue to rise at two to three times the rate of general inflation? As the following chapters will explain, a disturbing value equation is formed when consumers are isolated from the true cost of health care. When the only money that leaves their wallets is a $30 co-pay, how can they be expected to assign a realistic value to the service they've received? Many people think nothing of visiting their family doctors when they're feeling just a little under the weather. Instead of resting and seeking another option, they seek immediate assessment of their symptoms, which is the quickest way to drive up healthcare costs.

Every healthcare consumer is personally responsible for a small portion of our country's total healthcare spending, and individual users have the power to turn this troubling value equation around. When consumers are empowered to spend responsibly and take better care of themselves, total spending will slow down, ultimately reducing the inflation rate of premium increases. Employee engagement will translate into savings for both consumers and employers.

By offering employees choices and empowering them to make informed, responsible, and cost-conscious decisions about their lifestyles and their healthcare spending, you'll create a healthier, stronger workforce. You'll also be saving your company, yourself, and your employees—not to mention the entire country—a lot of money. It's time for consumers to become proactive about their healthcare spending by leveraging the unique value proposition of the consumer-driven health plan (CDHP) solution, an approach in which employees benefit through a low-premium, high-deductible health plan coupled with a personal healthcare account they can use to pay healthcare expenses not covered by insurance.

To energize employees about the CDHP solution, you must first help them improve their knowledge of healthcare costs. Once consumers become aware of the actual costs of the healthcare services they access, and are rewarded with incentives, they'll be more inclined to question the need to seek healthcare services in the first place and less inclined to make poor choices that lower their own quality of life and put a strain on both their budgets and the healthcare system. They'll also work toward understanding all their healthcare options, and choose the most appropriate, cost-effective options when it's time to do so.

Consumers may not be aware of the direct link between bad habits—such as tobacco and alcohol use, lack of physical exercise, and poor diet—and the steadily increasing cost of health care, but the reality is that these habits are a big part of the healthcare problem. Let's return to that car analogy for a moment. The top priority after buying a new car is maintenance. To keep the car in excellent shape, a maintenance schedule that includes regular oil changes and having the tires rotated is required. To prevent damage to the vehicle, you'll want to avoid accidents by not speeding and driving extra carefully when it's raining. If only most people gave their bodies the same consideration, we would be a much healthier nation!

Another important step toward reducing reliance on health care is building a culture of health and well-being in the workplace. This will help employees take better care of their health, and you'll see the benefits reflected in fewer visits to health services providers, fewer prescription drug purchases, and increased workplace productivity. We'll discuss this concept of well-being in greater depth in later chapters.

At the end of the day, the solution to the healthcare spending crisis in America rests with consumers—they have the ultimate voice. Until we engage, educate, and empower them, healthcare costs will continue to rise and the burden of treating preventable illnesses will continue to strain the system. Traditional health insurance options helped cause our current healthcare crisis. It is unrealistic—Einstein might even say insane—to expect the same options will solve the healthcare crisis. New thinking is required.

As this book goes to press, Congress and the White House are still evaluating the best ways to reform a healthcare system that just about everyone agrees is facing a deep crisis. We believe the large-scale solution to that crisis must embrace the five principles the Trump Administration put forward during the initial discussions about repealing the Affordable Care Act. Those principles are: affordability; accessibility; high-quality health care; incentivizing innovation; and empowering consumers through transparency and accountability. We believe those principles must not be forgotten, because they clearly show leaders in government, industry, and the media the best way forward on this issue.

In the meantime, as we await the substantial healthcare reform this country so desperately needs, we offer *Bend the Healthcare Trend* as a support to employers who seek to do just that: reverse the crippling cycle of cost increases that have such a powerfully negative financial impact on their companies and their employees. It's long past time for all of us to let our healthcare dollars do the talking by choosing the appropriate CDHP solution and putting the power back where it belongs: in the hands of the people.

1

The Primer

The Problem

Our healthcare costs are soaring. After many failed attempts to control these costs, it's time to rethink the term *health care* by putting more emphasis on health and less on care. A paradigm shift is needed, and this starts with each of us seeing ourselves as consumers of health care who are in control of what our dollars purchase, and not as patients who passively accept what's offered by physicians or an employer's health plan.

Health care and the means by which consumers access it have changed considerably in recent years, as has the level of information available to them and their families through technology. In recent years we have seen truly explosive growth in health information from the Internet, featuring everything from detailed health information service sites like WebMD.com and CDHPCoach.com to smaller healthcare blogs, sites that deliver the latest updates on new drug therapies, and websites that specialize in posting ratings of specific providers—not to mention the ongoing narrative by the mainstream media. You would think this ever-expanding avalanche of information would create an opportunity where consumers were better informed about their healthcare choices than ever before. Yet there are stubborn, persistent misconceptions about why health insurance costs continue to rise in this country.

Cumulative Increases in Health Insurance Premiums, General Annual Deductibles, and Workers' Earnings, 2006-2015

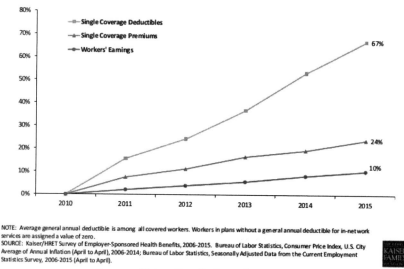

NOTE: Average general annual deductible is among all covered workers. Workers in plans without a general annual deductible for in-network services are assigned a value of zero.
SOURCE: Kaiser/HRET Survey of Employer-Sponsored Health Benefits, 2006-2015. Bureau of Labor Statistics, Consumer Price Index, U.S. City Average of Annual Inflation (April to April), 2006-2014; Bureau of Labor Statistics, Seasonally Adjusted Data from the Current Employment Statistics Survey, 2006-2015 (April to April).

Source: Kaiser Family Foundation, 2016.

The cost of health care today is borne collectively by the employer and the employee. According to the 2016 Milliman Medical Index, the total cost of health care for a typical family of four is shared by employers and employees. Each funding source can be defined by one of three main categories:

- **Employer contribution**. Employers that sponsor health plans subsidize the cost of health insurance for their employees by allocating compensation dollars to pay a substantial share of the cost. The portion paid by the employer typically varies according to the benefit plan option the employee selects and in most cases is approximately 60% of the total cost.

- **Employee contribution**. Employees who choose to participate in the employer's health benefit plan typically also pay a substantial portion of costs, usually through pretax payroll deductions (salary reduction).

- **Employee out-of-pocket cost at time of service**. When employees receive care, they pay for a portion of their care via health plan deductibles, co-pays, and coinsurance. While this exposure is capped by out-of-pocket maximums as legislated by federal law, these costs are still material to the employees and their families.

The typical family of four costs $25,826 annually in premium and out-of-pocket expenses, and the majority of costs are borne by the employer. In 2016, employers on average contributed 57% of costs, or $14,793, while employees paid the other 43%, or $6,717 in pretax contributions through payroll deductions and $4,316 in the form of out-of-pocket expenses incurred at time of service.[3]

The Cause

Healthcare trend is the healthcare industry's terminology for inflation, and it's primarily made up of two components: unit cost (the actual cost of healthcare products or services) and utilization (the number of times a healthcare product or service is purchased). For example a 10% trend means that a service or product that costs $10,000 this year would be $11,000 next year.

Consumers have a big role in getting national healthcare spending under control, but most healthcare users don't understand how their choices have contributed to the current challenge. This is because they don't understand the true costs of their lifestyle choices and the impact those choices have on the cost of health products and services. Consider how the cost of LASIK eye surgery has dropped in recent years, while per capita healthcare spending has increased exponentially.

LASIK is a common form of surgery for those individuals that need corrective vision support from wearing glasses or contacts. The actual procedure has evolved from a surgical correction that involved freezing the cornea before removing connective tissue, to the sophisticated application of today's advanced laser technology. With the constant evolution and positive outcomes, this surgery has become relatively common. According to the American Society of Cataract and Refractive Surgery, more than 28 million LASIK procedures have been done worldwide since 1990.

What is interesting about this type of treatment is that it is very seldom covered by any type of health insurance plan. The cost is borne by the individual and is considered elective surgery. The cost of the surgery varies by medical practice and the extent of the procedure. The cost of the procedure is transparent, and the consumer pays at the time of service. Because it is their money, consumers are unlikely to make an uninformed decision. You would think there would be a parallel between the cost of a specific procedure and the rise in overall healthcare spending, but that isn't the case. Broadly speaking, the cost of LASIK surgery has dropped over the years. According to Market Scope Research, in 2016 the average cost of LASIK was $3,680 compared to $4,360 in 1998. What causes such a discrepancy in healthcare spending? The root of the problem is the uninformed healthcare consumer and a lack of transparency in cost and quality by the "rulemakers:" government, big hospital systems, big pharmaceutical companies, and health insurance carriers. The lesson here is clear. Medical procedures paid for with consumers' hard-earned money should be carefully researched, considered, and evaluated against other options. That's what an informed healthcare consumer does.

In practice, though, most consumers are unaware of the actual costs of the healthcare services covered by their insurance plans, and all too often they are led to believe that the more expensive care they receive, the better that care is going to be. Sadly, there is little correlation between price and quality of care. When billing and payment are arranged between providers (hospitals, doctors, and pharmaceutical companies) and insurance companies, consumers don't think twice about going to the doctor or getting a prescription filled. For most consumers, it's just a co-pay.

Simply put, when there isn't transparency and a real cost associated with medical care, consumers won't take the time to consider the cost or whether they really need the service they're seeking or if there is a better alternative. This kind of behavior leads to unnecessary use of the healthcare system and drives up cost. Of course, no one should be discouraged from getting the care and medication they really need. Most treatments are medically necessary. But just as you shouldn't go to the plastic surgeon on a whim, you shouldn't go to the doctor every time you have the sniffles. Consumers have little control over some factors contributing to healthcare costs; however, we all have quite a bit of control over the lifestyle choices we make every day. Common lifestyle choices that can put the consumer at risk include the following:

- Lack of physical activity

- Poor nutrition (e.g., high fat, low fiber)

- High-risk recreational activity

- Ineffective stress management

- Tobacco use

- Lack of sleep

- Overuse of alcohol

In turn, these poor lifestyle choices can lead to preventable chronic or life-threatening diseases such as diabetes, heart disease, cancer, and stroke.

Medical studies show that adults with common chronic medical conditions can improve their health significantly by participating in lifestyle change programs. Programs such as nutritional counseling, exercise training, stress management, and smoking cessation can assist patients in living a healthier life. Doctors often advise that patients adopt such lifestyle changes, yet doing so and following through to make the changes needed to sustain a healthier life is always up to the patient, and is dependent on factors such as desire, willpower, and peer support.

The Current Solution

Managed care hasn't ignored the issue of rising healthcare spending, but for the most part, the managed care strategy has run its course and in many cases is not succeeding in holding down costs. Traditional health plans rely on a managed-care structure whose primary aim is to control rising healthcare costs by focusing on preventive care and physician-driven decision-making. It's a supply-side economic approach to managing costs. Traditional managed care's many cost-reduction techniques have included offering economic incentives to physicians for selecting less costly forms of care, controlling inpatient admissions and the length of hospital stays, and, in some cases, withholding care. Initially, managed care held down costs through this method, but over time, healthcare consumers pushed back because they didn't want insurance companies dictating their medical care providers or treatment options. The power of choice had been all but taken away from consumers.

The difference between using traditional managed-care techniques to reduce costs and helping consumers monitor their own behaviors and healthcare spending is driven by one major factor: motive. Consumers are focused on saving money, especially when it's their own. Their focus on money is tempered by attention to their health. By becoming better informed healthcare consumers and making good lifestyle choices, consumers not only avoid using the system unnecessarily but also guarantee their health is the number one priority for them and their families. That mind-set benefits the consumers, their employers, and the insurance companies who are underwriting their risk.

A New Approach

When consumers are uninformed about the causes of increased healthcare spending, how can they understand how they might address the root of the problem? If their spending remains unchecked, healthcare costs will continue to rise faster and higher than income levels and the general rate of inflation, reaching cost levels that employers and the government can't support. The only reasonable alternative is to consider an engaged approach to health insurance—consumer-driven health plans and worksite well-being.

Consumer-driven health plans are health insurance plans that combine a lower premium higher-deductible health plan (HDHP) with a healthcare account. The tax-preferred money contributed to a healthcare account, combined with some out-of-pocket expenses, covers healthcare spending up to the amount of the annual deductible. This health insurance solution is highly effective because of its philosophy, which is governed by three principles: transparency, responsibility, and opportunity.

Principle One: Transparency

In a traditional health insurance plan, a typical user goes to a health services provider without considering the visit's actual cost (contracted rate). In most cases, all the consumer pays is a small portion of the cost of the service in the form of a co-pay. The inherent design of this health insurance product hides the rest of the cost from the consumer. Without knowing the true costs, consumers have no incentive to consider their options and choose the most appropriate, cost-effective treatment.

On the other hand, CDHPs promote transparency. Consumers are encouraged to seek out information such as the cost of health services and the range of alternative treatments. This helps them make the most informed and effective choices. After a user accesses a healthcare service, the health insurance company sends an explanation of benefits (EOB), which details the cost of the service in the form of a cost breakdown. Consumers see exactly where each part of their healthcare dollar is spent, and who is responsible for paying the cost. Unlike users of traditional health insurance plans, CDHP users understand the true cost and value of the health services they receive.

Principle Two: Responsibility

With knowledge comes responsibility. Once consumers know the value of the health services they receive, it's up to them to make informed decisions about how they use them, and to do whatever they can to avoid needing them in the first place. A responsible decision about using health services could be as simple as speaking to a nurse or taking a day off work to rest instead of making a trip to the doctor. In most cases, consumers can access the health insurance company's nurse help lines for medical advice instead of going to the emergency room for non-emergencies. The help lines are staffed by registered nurses specifically trained to answer symptom-based questions and provide guidance. Direct primary care, telemedicine, and urgent care facilities are other resources that can help to identify true emergencies from the day-to-day lumps, bumps, aches, and pains – importantly, at a fraction of the cost of an emergency room visit.

To avoid needing these services at all, it's the consumer's responsibility to take appropriate measures to maintain good health. These decisions can include washing hands more frequently during flu season; cutting back on high-cholesterol, high-fat, and low-fiber foods; and working some physical activity into the daily routine. When consumers make responsible decisions by educating themselves about the real cost of health services and by consistently seeking preventive care on their own, the burden on the healthcare system becomes much lighter.

Principle Three: Opportunity

The CDHP solution comes with opportunities for the consumer to benefit physically and financially. Beyond improving the consumer's health and general well-being, participating in a CDHP offers significant financial advantages to the consumer in the form of unused dollars, which can be carried forward for future healthcare expenses.

CDHP Components

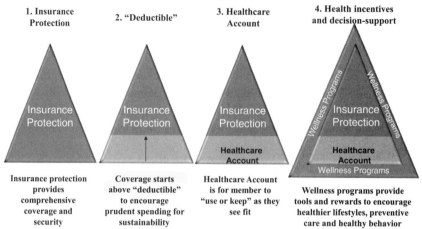

1. Insurance Protection	2. "Deductible"	3. Healthcare Account	4. Health incentives and decision-support
Insurance protection provides comprehensive coverage and security	Coverage starts above "deductible" to encourage prudent spending for sustainability	Healthcare Account is for member to "use or keep" as they see fit	Wellness programs provide tools and rewards to encourage healthier lifestyles, preventive care and healthy behavior

Let's say the deductible for a single employee is $1,500. You, as the employer and provider of health insurance, might contribute $750 into a healthcare account, a tax-preferred contribution. Your employees can use your contribution to pay for eligible medical expenses, and if they're prudent with those funds, they may not incur additional out-of-pocket expenses beyond the premium paid to purchase the health plan. If they don't spend the employer's healthcare account allocation, they can save it for future healthcare expenses by rolling it over from one year to the next. We call this financial benefit to the consumer the rollover effect, a powerful incentive to manage healthcare account dollars wisely.

Consumers who participate in a CDHP also have comprehensive protection when they need it most. If they spend the full $750, the next $750 would come out of their pocket, and then the HDHP coverage kicks in, covering most eligible medical expenses above the $1,500 deductible when it's structured with a high level of coinsurance (i.e., 100% or 90% paid by the health plan).

Even in catastrophic situations that cause a CDHP member's healthcare spending to exceed the annual deductible, there can be significant savings for the employer and the employee through lower premiums and comprehensive coverage.

The good news is that exceeding a $1,500 deductible isn't all that likely. By engaging in the first two CDHP principles—transparency and responsibility—most employees should be able to avoid using up their health-care accounts. More often than not, there will be money left over at the end of the year, and that's when even more benefits kick in. The money that isn't used up over the course of the year can roll over to the next year. This process can continue indefinitely and create a financial benefit in subsequent years. The difference between paying a traditional insurance premium and investing in a healthcare account can be compared to the difference between paying rent and buying a house. If you can afford either, why spend your money on something that offers you no return on your investment?

Get Involved

As providers of health insurance, employers must ask themselves whether they want to engage their employees in the process of controlling healthcare costs, and whether they're comfortable encouraging employees to manage their own healthcare accounts. If these sound like steps in the right direction, CDHPs represent an engaged healthcare option that curbs costs through education, behavior change, and encouraging wellness. Below are some advantages you may expect from a CDHP:

- **Comprehensive coverage, including preventive care.** Employees in CDHPs continue to receive recommended care at the same or higher levels as those in traditional plans. Preventive care visits increase for those in CDHPs because there's a financial incentive to stay healthy. CDHP plan members have regular checkups, physicals, and preventive health screenings.

- **Preferred provider organization (PPO) benefits.** A PPO is an orga-nized network of doctors, hospitals, and other medical providers who agree to offer their services to an insurer's clients at a discounted fee for each service – and no balance bill beyond that agreed-upon rate. It offers employees a list of doctors and hospitals that could save them money, and they won't need a referral to visit a new doctor, as a tradi-tional managed-care product requires.

- **Rewards for healthy lifestyles.** Good health is priceless! The biggest step toward reducing reliance on health care is to improve employ-ees' overall health and well-being. By achieving this goal and main-taining positive results, employees will be healthier and reduce their healthcare spending. They may also earn rewards and incentives from their health plan provider.

- **The rollover effect.** Rollover funds are the engine of change in a CDHP because they help consumers save unused benefit dollars from year to year. These tax-preferred dollars accumulate until account holders are ready to use them.

According to a recent Kaiser Health Benefits survey, 13% of covered workers were enrolled in some sort of high-deductible health plan in 2010. By 2014, that number had risen to 20% of covered workers, an increase of more than 50%.[4] This growing market share highlights the importance of better understanding the trends in spending and utilization for CDHP consumers, and how they compare to their non-CDHP counterparts. To encourage employees to improve health and lifestyle choices, the SHRM 2015 Employee Benefits research report, released on June 29, 2015, found that 70% of US employers currently offer a general wellness program, up from 58% in 2008, when SHRM first surveyed companies on preventive health and wellness benefits.[5]

Employers across the country are recognizing that CDHPs are a reasonable answer to the deep problems plaguing the American healthcare system. It's time for companies of all sizes to choose a more cost-effective approach to health care and help change the system for the better … by making it about the people.

Increase in CDHP Market Share

Sharp increase in offerings of consumer-directed health plans

Percent of employers offering/likely to offer CDHP by employer size

Number of employees	2010	2011	2012	2013	2014	Very likely to offer in 2017
All employers (10+ employees)	17%	20%	22%	23%	27%	36%
All large employers (500+ employees)	23%	32%	36%	39%	48%	66%
Jumbo employers (20,000+ employees)	51%	48%	59%	63%	72%	88%

Source: 2016 Mercer's National Survey of Employer-Sponsored Health Plans

Case Study: *All-Access Pass*

Cindy was a healthy, fifty-three-year-old grandmother who worked as a business officer for an independent private school in Maine. As part of the decision-making team that chose to switch the school's health insurance plan from a traditional HMO product to a CDHP, she was a well-informed user of her CDHP.

Cindy began suffering from severe migraines. After reviewing her physician options in her PPO, she found a physician in her area and booked an appointment. The physician wasn't overly concerned with Cindy's headaches and advised her to "wait and see." After a few months of waiting and seeing, Cindy's headaches weren't getting any better. Still in pain and unwilling to accept her physician's lack of response, Cindy put her CDHP to use.

The product design uses a PPO, which gives Cindy access to an extensive network of healthcare providers, both in and outside of Maine. After doing some research, Cindy booked an appointment with a nationally recognized expert in Boston, Massachusetts. She was soon diagnosed with a potentially fatal brain aneurysm, and, within two weeks, was undergoing life- saving surgery at Brigham and Women's Hospital in Boston. Had Cindy continued to assume the passive approach of her first physician, it's likely that her condition would have become fatal. As a CDHP member, however, she had access to specialists outside of her home state, allowing her to get the treatment she needed.

Cindy's total medical expenses exceeded $100,000. Her deductible was $3,000, and her employer covered 50% of it through the health-care account, exposing Cindy to a maximum out-of-pocket portion of $1,500. After she paid that, her CDHP fully covered the remaining cost. Cindy's CDHP not only gave her the peace of mind that came from knowing that her financial obligation was completely manageable, but it also saved her life.

2

The CDHP Value Proposition

Consumer Skepticism

All innovative products and services have to overcome some hurdles when first introduced to the market, and CDHPs are no different. Americans have been subscribing to the same type of health insurance programs for more than twenty-five years, and much of their effectiveness at holding costs down has run its course. The US healthcare system has changed significantly over the past several decades, as have consumers' knowledge and sensitivity to healthcare costs. CDHPs take those changes into consideration.

When something is new and different, people tend to be skeptical, especially when it offers a solution to a problem that seems impossible to fix. What do consumers who are still using traditional managed-care plans know about CDHPs? Ask most people, and you'd probably find their answer is based on uninformed media influence, negative perception, and general misgivings that tend to surround new products and services. Unfortunately, the negative publicity gives them a somewhat skewed perception of this innovative approach to health insurance.

One of the most common misperceptions about CDHPs is that they're only HDHPs. This tells only half the story. An HDHP without a healthcare account covers users only when they've incurred significant costs. The engine of the CDHP is a healthcare account, which helps the consumer understand the true cost of health care and contains the funds that pay for their healthcare products and services.

The principles of transparency, responsibility, and opportunity define this new approach to health insurance. The employer, consumer, provider, and health plan all play a significant role, and those roles must be understood for a CDHP to deliver on its value proposition. So what exactly does the CDHP value proposition entail?

high deductible health plan

Engaging Healthcare Consumers

A CDHP is made up of two equally important parts: a lower premium HDHP and a healthcare account. The HDHP is sometimes referred to as catastrophic insurance because the deductibles are, by definition, higher than those of most health insurance plans ($1,500 or more) and they generally ask consumers to pay part of the cost of healthcare products and services before insurance coverage kicks in. With the HDHP's premium savings and transparency, employers can redirect premium dollars into healthcare accounts and engage their employees by providing them with dollars to pay for their medical expenses.

With CDHPs, a significant portion of the money employers and employees save on their insurance premiums can be contributed directly into the other important component of the CDHP, the healthcare account. The healthcare account is a tax-advantaged vehicle that is used to pay for qualified medical expenses and is sheltered from federal and, in most cases, state income tax (the exceptions being Alabama, California and New Jersey). Consumers can choose how this money should be spent or saved, and how they want to proceed when or if the time comes to access the funds.

Healthcare accounts offer consumers a new way to pay for health care. They allow them to make decisions without having to consult an insurer or a third party and to pay for current medical expenses while possibly saving for future ones, all on a tax-preferred basis. The best part is that if you live a healthy and responsible lifestyle and don't need to spend your money on medical expenses, it's yours to use in the future. If it's not spent, it doesn't go into someone else's pocket like the money you've been contributing to traditional insurance plans.

Advantages of CDHPs

One of the CDHP features is the lower premium, higher front-end deductible. Though some consumers shy away from a higher deductible at first, assuming they'll be paying more for their health care out of pocket, it's worth their while to review the benefits and do the math. The main appeal of higher deductibles is that they can significantly lower premiums—by as much as 20% to 25% in the first year and lower rates of increase from year to year thereafter. Ideally, an employer should redirect at least 50% of the premium savings toward helping employees set up and fund healthcare accounts.

Aside from lowering premiums, higher deductibles create transparency. Each time the consumer accesses the healthcare system, he or she receives an explanation of benefits. This, as noted earlier, is a statement sent by the health insurance company that lists various details such as costs of healthcare services received and who is responsible for payment: the consumer, the insurer, or the healthcare provider. The EOB provides a lot of useful information that helps consumers track their medical expenses and total out-of-pocket costs for health care. It may be the first time a consumer sees the actual costs of all aspects of a visit or a medical procedure -- not just what they pay. The healthcare delivery system resists transparency of cost and quality information; it isn't readily available to consumers at the point of service like most material items and services are today. In health care funded by a CDHP plan, it becomes clear that health care is expensive. Most people who open their EOB statement are shocked by the billed charges and the actual contracted net cost of the services, as well as the cost variation by locationCDHP plans are designed to encourage consumers to seek information about the cost of healthcare services ahead of time so they can make informed choices. One area that often leads to a huge financial surprise for consumers is the use of an emergency room, especially when it is used for the treatment of nonemergency conditions. Emergency rooms are designed to deal with sudden and serious accidents and illness (e.g., being shot, being stabbed, bleeding profusely, suffering severe head trauma or chest pain, and so on). Yet a significant portion of emergency room visitors do not need urgent care.[6]

According to the National Health Statistics report issued by the Department of Health and Human Services, approximately 20% of US adults seek health care at the emergency room each year, a percentage that has remained largely unchanged for more than a decade. In 2014, of patients who used the emergency room, only 18% of adults visiting the ER on more than one occasion cited the seriousness of the medical problem as the reason for the visit. Of those who visited, 12% said it was because their doctor's office was not open and 7% lacked access to a personal physician and used the emergency room as their primary source of healthcare services.

Since consumers share financial responsibility with a CDHP, they benefit by considering other alternatives for seeking health care. For example:

- **Urgent care centers.** These are clinics that can usually handle problems that need immediate attention but aren't life-threatening or emergencies, such as stitches, sprains, and X-rays.

- **Retail health clinics.** Many major pharmacies and retail stores, such as Target, CVS, or Walgreens, now have walk-in clinics staffed by medical professionals. Consumers visit when it is convenient, and typically seek treatment for coughs, infections, and flu shots.

- **Walk-in and extended hours at doctors' offices.** Many doctors' offices offer open appointment times and extended hours for consultations.

- **Telemedicine.** Technology is bringing medicine into our homes as consumers connect with physicians 24/7 using mobile communications like Skype or FaceTime.

- **Direct primary care.** Through a direct-to-consumer contracted relationship with a primary care doctor, consumers avoid typical fee-for-service charges in favor of a monthly membership fee. In exchange, consumers enjoy 24/7 access to their PCP, discounted ancillary services, and a set number of face-to-face visits with the PCP for medical care.

When consumers see their EOBs and the actual cost of provider visits, it engages them in the true cost of health care. They begin to understand that today's claims are tomorrow's higher premiums. Under the traditional managed-care co-pay structure, consumers are charged a nominal co-pay (a small percentage of the actual cost) each time they use the healthcare system and are not informed of the other costs. It is the primary reason why consumers are desensitized to the cost of healthcare services when they only have to pick up a small percentage of the tab.

The constant reminder of where their money is spent is an excellent preventive measure for overspending. The EOB statements encourage consumers to take advantage of all the education, tools, and preventive care at their disposal as CDHP members. They also have the ability to lower their out-of-pocket costs and maximize their rollover opportunities by making more informed healthcare decisions.

Sample EOB Statement

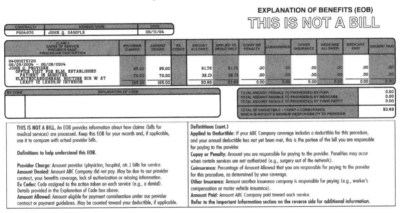

Informed Decisions

The CDHP solution focuses so strongly on avoiding unnecessary healthcare costs that some employers worry that consumers will avoid accessing necessary care in order to save money. Of course, CDHPs have several features in place to help prevent this from becoming an issue. One feature in particular eases many people's worries: you're the boss and in full control, and taking better care of yourself is one of the CDHP solution's fundamental principles.

Cost-cutting is an issue for all health insurance plans, but what differentiates health plans is the way they approach the cuts. Decision makers at traditional insurance plans decide where money should be saved and where it should be spent. Basically, they decide what kinds of services they will pay for and what facilities the consumer will be able to access. In a CDHP, it's your money and your decision. When you've been experiencing a terrible pain in your abdomen for several days, wouldn't you want full control over your treatment plan and physician selection versus the insurer making that decision for you?

CDHPs encourage broad consumer education and more healthcare choices so users can make informed decisions in times of illness and stress—or, even better, before health problems occur.

The following points illustrate some ways in which CDHP users behave differently from users of traditional insurance plans:

- **Routine annual physicals and preventive care.** CDHP members are more likely than traditional health insurance subscribers to participate in health and well-being programs if offered. The point of routine annual physicals is to catch problems early, and the aim of preventive care is to minimize the risk of developing problematic health conditions in the first place. Preventive care services include screening for diseases, immunizations, and counseling on disease prevention. CDHP members are educated about the importance of preventive health care and catching conditions early, and they understand that the earlier you catch something, the less money you'll spend on treatment.

There are pre-existing conditions for various health concerns that illustrate the power of early detection. For example, Joanne was unaware that she had developed a slightly misshapen mole on her lower back. She visited her doctor only to address specific problems, never for a regular physical, and because she didn't know about her mole, her doctor remained unaware of it. Years later, the cells of her mole are found to be cancerous, and doctors are worried that the cancer may have spread to Joanne's other organs via her bloodstream or lymphatic system. Joanne needs the mole removed, and treatment will likely require surgery, radiation therapy, and possibly even chemotherapy. Had her doctor noticed the mole earlier, he probably would have recommended removing it as a precaution. A simple yearly checkup could have saved Joanne not only all the cost associated with treatment but also the risks to her life and her general state of health.

Ruby, a mother of three young children, is a good example of using preventive care wisely. At the beginning of every winter, Ruby takes her kids to get flu shots, which will decrease their chances of getting the flu. Their potential good health also ensures they won't pass the flu along to any of their classmates at school or day care, to each other, or to their aging grandparents.

- **Treatment programs.** CDHP consumers have a shared responsibility for their healthcare spending. Therefore, they have an incentive to make prudent and cost-conscious choices when utilizing healthcare services. According to a recent Rand Health survey, families that switched from a traditional health insurance plan to a CDHP spent on average 21% less on health care. Two-thirds of the savings came from initiating fewer episodes of care, and one-third came from spending less per episode.

One of the fastest growing areas of healthcare spending is prescription drugs, especially specialty drugs. According to the Milliman Medical Index (MMI), prescription drugs now make up 17% of the total healthcare money spent, of which specialty drugs make up 35% and are rapidly growing in proportion to total healthcare costs. Of course, CDHP members have choices to consider when taking medications, and it is important that routine maintenance medications be taken consistently to avoid any serious condition at a later point. The ramifications of noncompliance when it comes to maintenance medications can be serious, leading to expensive future treatments that could have been avoided. For example, consider Andre, an asthma sufferer, who has a prescription inhaler that he's supposed to use twice a day. Not having had an attack for a few weeks, he decides he probably doesn't need his inhaler as often and will use it only if he feels an attack coming on. However, asthma doesn't always work this way, so when Andre does have an attack, immediately using his inhaler doesn't stop it. He's rushed to the hospital, where he has to undergo tests and spend the night, resulting in a significant hospital bill. If he'd done what his doctor recommended and used his inhaler as prescribed, his only bill would have been to refill his prescription.

- **Asking questions.** CDHP members are more likely to ask about medical costs and choose a less expensive option with the same or better quality outcome. This makes sense because consumers spend their own money more wisely than they spend their employer's money. Usually, healthcare consumers don't ask if there's an effective, less expensive alternative to the treatment being prescribed. Patients should follow their doctors' treatment plans, but this doesn't mean they shouldn't ask if there are less expensive alternatives. It never hurts to ask.

Tom, for example, suffers from epilepsy. His doctor has prescribed a drug called Depakene, which Tom takes three times a day. One bottle of Depakene lasts one month and costs him $494.13. If Tom had asked a few questions, he would have found out that 250 milligrams of valproic acid, which is the common generic alternative and is essentially the same drug, can be purchased for $35.67. This is a 721% price difference, one that isn't uncommon between generic and brand-name drugs. Choosing the generic alternative would have saved Tom $5,501.52 per year in unnecessary costs.

- **Alternative choices**. CDHP members are encouraged to be responsible healthcare consumers. They become more aware and more conscious of which symptoms and degrees of ill- ness require a visit to the emergency room or family doctor, and which they can safely treat themselves. When they aren't sure, there are options to consider in order to determine the urgency of treatment needed, such as a health plan nurse advice line or telemedicine where they can use Skype or Facetime to find out whether their symptoms are serious.

Alternative measures that can take some of the burden off the healthcare system can be seen in Maria's example. Maria started feeling under the weather on Sunday afternoon, bothered by a runny nose and sore throat. She woke up Monday morning feeling the same and decided to call in sick to work. After calling, she took two acetaminophen tablets and went back to bed. Throughout the day, she drank tea, ate soup, and rested, and then took two more acetaminophen tablets in the afternoon. After a solid night's sleep, she woke up Tuesday morning feeling much better and went to work. Had Maria been worried about her symptoms, she could have called a nurse advice line, and may have been reassured that she was taking the right steps and that her symptoms were the signs of a common cold.

Another scenario: what if Maria was impatient by nature and her inclination was not to wait for her symptoms to subside? In this example, she wanted to be absolutely sure she wasn't suffering from something more serious and made an appointment to see her doctor that afternoon. Had this been the case, she wouldn't have given her body the rest it badly needed because she would have been too busy driving to the doctor's office and sitting in the waiting room when she could have been in bed, resting.

These examples demonstrate that under a CDHP, consumers get necessary and high-quality medical care when they need it. Doctors, medication, and hospitals are as available to them as to any other insured person. The difference is that the coverage is designed to get you to think before you spend, focus your healthcare dollars on what's really essential, and prevent you from wasting hard-earned money on avoidable costs.

Case Study: *Bending the Healthcare Trend by Moving the CDHP Levers*

ABC Engineering employs over 600 people and is nationally recognized for the work of its consulting engineers and scientists. They are experts in providing innovative solutions to complicated geotechnical issues. The key to their success is the focus and commitment to their talented team of employees.

ABC followed a traditional approach when moving away from a fully insured medical plan to a CDHP using a health savings account (HSA).

Several years before ABC adopted a CDHP with a health savings account, the company offered a non-qualified high-deductible health plan, coupled with a health reimbursement arrangement (HRA). ABC funded the HRA at 100% of the deductible to reimburse employees for out-of-pocket medical expenses subject to their plan's deductible. With no responsibility for the exposure to their deductible, employees and their families had little to no incentive to change their behavior—all medical expenses were covered in full. As time went by, healthcare costs increased and ABC's health insurance premiums rose by double digits each year.

ABC's new strategic advisor recommended an innovative engaged approach to managing healthcare costs. The recommendation was to move away from a non-qualified deductible health plan paired with an HRA and to offer a CDHP coupled with a health savings account (HSA). HSAs are tax-advantaged medical savings accounts available to employees who are enrolled in a qualified high-deductible health plan. The funds deposited in the HSA are not subject to FICA, federal or state income taxes (except Alaska, California, and New Jersey) at the time of deposit if done through payroll. If the employee chooses to make deposits to the HSA on an after-tax basis, the same rules apply, with the exception that FICA taxes have already been paid. In a CDHP paired with an HSA, once the employer commits to funding the HSA, the employee owns the money by law regardless of whether she ever makes a claim.

continued

Under the new plan, ABC's employees would be allowed to save for their own healthcare expenses. With the move from the HRA to the HSA healthcare account model, ABC covered 65% of the employee's deductible exposure. The deductible was set at $2,000 for an individual and $4,000 for a family. These deductibles applied to all healthcare services, excluding preventive care services, which were covered at 100%.

ABC's transition to a CDHP paired with an HSA was staged, taking place over several years. In adopting the change, the company made it clear that the CDHP was the direction that made the most sense for both the company and its employees over the long term. While making this transition to a full-replacement CDHP, ABC also offered a plan with a very low deductible ($250 for an individual, $500 for a family). That plan limited out-of-pocket exposure and was less work for the employees. It was also much more expensive in the form of higher premiums. ABC set its premium contribution strategy targeted on the CDHP and allowed the employees to choose the lower deductible, higher premium plan at an additional cost.

CHDPs paired with HSAs have some guidelines that specify who can and can't enroll in an HSA. To address employees who aren't eligible under law, ABC offered an accommodation CDHP with an HRA for those who were enrolled by Medicare, covered by a spouse's plan, enrolled in a flexible spending account (FSA), or received veterans' benefits three months before enrollment.

The result of all this careful planning was dramatic. Fully 85% of ABC's employees chose the CHDP/HSA plan in the very first year. The remaining 15% either weren't eligible and enrolled in the accommodation plan or chose to pay the higher premium for the lower deductible plan.

ABC's leadership team envisioned a five-year trajectory for the plan. Funding the HSA at 65% of the full deductible was viewed as an investment with a high probability of a favorable return in the form of strong employee engagement and the rollover effect. Shifts in employee behavior would result in substantial improvements in cost control over time. With that goal in mind, the leadership team made communication and education a high priority.

continued

ABC worked closely with its strategic advisor to develop a comprehensive plan for educating the workforce. ABC employees learned how to make more informed decisions as healthcare consumers. They gained an understanding of the need to research such things as cost, quality, and value before committing to a course of treatment. They also learned insights on what levels of treatment and care were needed when certain health-related situations arose. A few examples: They learned the difference between seeking treatment in an outpatient clinic rather than an emergency room; using telemedicine rather than a walk-in clinic; or even using a freestanding medical imaging center rather than purchasing medical imaging in a hospital setting.

To enhance the member education process, ABC sent out bi-weekly communications on important topics for employees so they could become more educated consumers of their healthcare options. For instance, one such communication piece offered resources and information for weight loss and maintaining an ideal body weight.

Today, ABC is focused on an ongoing strategy to keep employees engaged so they can be better healthcare consumers. To help them, ABC introduced Captivated Health Concierge, a 24/7 healthcare decision-support program for employees and their families. When employees on ABC's CDHP/HSA plan need information, they can call the concierge for guidance and information. They also have access to a mobile application through this service that contains all their personal health insurance information and helpful tools and resources.

The careful planning and execution paid off. Employees have embraced these initiatives, and behaviors are changing—and after years of double-digit premium increases under its low-deductible, HRA-only plan, ABC's cost increase in the first year after the change was just 2%. The following year, the total cost changed 0% and in following years actually decreased by 3% in a market where cost increases for employers of this size are typically going up at 6.5%–10% per year!

ABC's story illustrates an exciting possibility: significantly better cost control is achieved when companies move to CDHPs and support employees and their families as they take on a deeper, more informed personal role in their healthcare decisions.

3

The CDHP Engine—
Healthcare Account
Structures

Plan Mechanics

The pairing of a healthcare account and an HDHP is common to all CDHPs. The differences become apparent in the ways each healthcare account operates. There are three types of CDHP healthcare account structures, each with its own unique benefits and limitations: flexible spending accounts (FSAs), health reimbursement arrangements (HRAs), and health savings accounts (HSAs).

Flexible Spending Accounts (FSAs)—The Health
Dollar Maximizer™

A flexible spending account is a good first step toward a CDHP because it teaches consumers how to fund and manage a healthcare account. An FSA introduces employees to the healthcare account structure, which has them fund the account with their own money, deducted from their paychecks on a pretax basis (salary reduction). Then FSAs require consumers to manage that account effectively to increase the purchasing power of their healthcare dollars.

The FSA enables employees to pay for qualified medical expenses on a tax-preferred basis, as defined in Section 213(d) of the Internal Revenue Service (IRS) code. Essentially, it lowers the cost of medical services by the amount of your tax rate or, on average, by 33%. As long as the money is spent on qualified medical expenses, the money used to pay for those services isn't subject to income tax, a benefit that amounts to substantial savings. Employers benefit from this plan through a reduction of 7.65% (6.2% for Social Security and 1.45% for Medicare) in their Federal Insurance Contributions Act (FICA) tax expense. It is important to note that if the legal structure of your company is an S Corporation, LLC, or partnership, shareholders owning more than 2% of the company are not eligible to participate.

The FSA provides first-dollar coverage, which means the funds for reimbursement are available on the effective date of the plan, even though the account hasn't been funded yet by the employee. In other words, the employer provides an FSA credit line to the employee and advances funds to pay for qualified medical expenses right away. This feature is a boon to employees who don't have to accrue significant savings before they're able to use medical services, but it does pose a certain risk to employers.

For example, an employee who has elected to contribute $1,000 toward his or her FSA might incur a $400 medical bill on the first day of the plan year. If the employee works at the company long enough to contribute $1,000 to the FSA, the credit line is paid up. If the employee leaves the company before contributing the full amount, the employer has no recourse to collect the unfunded balance. On the other hand, if the employee pays $1,000 into the FSA and spends only $600 before the end of the plan year, the positive balance reverts back to the employer to offset administrative costs.

FSA Contribution Strategy

Employees select an annual amount of money that the employer deducts from their paychecks before tax (salary reduction), and that amount is deposited into an account typically managed by the employee and a third-party administrator (TPA).

The single biggest drawback of the FSA for employees is the "use it or lose it" rule. The end-of-year balances of FSAs don't roll over, so the money employees don't spend over the course of the year is lost to them. In this way, the FSA scenario is similar to traditional health care—the user pays a certain amount without necessarily incurring equal medical costs. This is the least attractive feature of the FSA and sets the stage for the CDHP's "use it or keep it" value proposition.

Health Reimbursement Arrangements (HRAs)—The Health Dollar Value Builder™

A health reimbursement arrangement (HRA) is the next logical step in the consumerism model of a CDHP after an FSA. HRAs introduce the principle of "use it or keep it," and are employer-funded accounts used to reimburse employees for out-of-pocket healthcare expenses. The HRAs are notional accounts that have no actual cash value. Instead, they come with a promise to pay—the employer offers the employee an amount of credit toward the cost of the employee's medical expenses each year if he or she incurs a qualified medical expense.

With the HRA, decisions about structure, such as funding amount, rules of reimbursement, and rollover, are left up to the employer. The employer determines whether employees can build value in the healthcare account through a rollover that accumulates any positive balances from one year to the next. The employer also decides how much money rolls over from year to year by determining whether the rollover is a fixed amount, a percentage of the deductible, or capped at the deductible.

If an employee accumulates enough rollover to reach his or her deductible, you, as an employer, have two choices: You can cap the rollover at the deductible, ensuring that the employee is covered for all medical costs below the deductible. Or you can offer an enhanced benefit by allowing rollover balances to accumulate above the deductible and allow those dollars to be used for additional qualified medical expenses not covered by your health plan. The money in the HRA isn't actual cash that your employees have to invest, but credit you're giving them to pay for qualified medical expenses. Some examples of services typically not covered on a traditional plan, but that could be paid by an HRA, include dental care, orthodontics, or LASIK eye surgery.

Like FSAs, HRAs provide first-dollar coverage, so employees have the full amount of credit at their disposal on the first day of enrollment. Unlike with FSAs, this credit doesn't belong to the employee. This feature is a more conservative proposition for the employer—if employees leave the company, the account isn't portable and there's no balance that they can take with them. The credit is structured as a promise to pay until the funds are required. Most CFO's like the idea of such an inherent reserve.

The return on investment for the employer is twofold: First, the "use it or keep it" principle improves employees' knowledge of healthcare costs and improves their use of healthcare services. Second, employers can use HRAs to self-fund part of their employees' risk (i.e., out-of-pocket costs) and lower healthcare costs by leveraging deductibles and HRA funding from year to year, lowering overall health insurance costs.

HRA Contribution Strategy

Typically, an HRA is paired with a lower premium HDHP, and the employer funds an HRA to help employees pay some portion of the deductible—usually 50% or more. For example, an employer may agree to cover up to $750 of a $1,500 deductible. The employee is responsible for any expenses that are over this credit but below the deductible: the remaining $750. The employer doesn't have to pay into a fund for reimbursement, but reimburses medical costs as they occur. Any money the employer actually spends is treated like a health insurance premium and is a tax-deductible expense.

Employees can't contribute to HRAs themselves, but they can participate in an FSA at the same time to cover eligible healthcare expenses on a tax-preferred basis once their HRA funds are exhausted.

Health Savings Accounts (HSAs)—
The Health Dollar Equity Builder™

Lastly, a health savings account (HSA) is the purest form of CDHP. HSAs can be funded by an employer, by an employee, or both. The money is deposited into a bank account and is tax-preferred, much as in the other CDHP healthcare account structures. You are permitted to make a tax-free rollover from your IRA to an HSA only once in your lifetime, and the amount is limited to the maximum HSA contribution for the year, minus any contributions you've already made for the year..

HSAs are governed by the IRS, who determines who is and isn't eligible, as well as the rules and regulations regarding the funding and spending of the money in the HSA. For example, individuals who can be claimed as a dependent, who are enrolled in an FSA or in Medicare, or who have received veterans' benefits within the last three months are not eligible to establish an HSA.

Another important aspect of the HSA law that differentiates it from FSAs and HRAs is that consumers must purchase a qualified high-deductible health plan (QHDHP) in order to establish and fund an HSA. What this means is that the QHDHP must meet certain deductible and maximum out-of-pocket limitation requirements. For 2017, the IRS stipulated that the minimum deductibles for HSA account holders must be no less than $1,300 for a single person and $2,600 for a family of two or more. The maximum annual out-of-pocket expense is $6,650 for a single person and $13,100 for a family of two or more; the maximum amounts that can be contributed are $3,400 and $6,750, respectively. These amounts are indexed each year. (Note: As this book goes to press, the American Healthcare Act legislation passed by the House of Representatives would change this contribution cap to match the out-of-pocket maximums.)

A significant difference between HSAs and other CDHP healthcare account structures is that the account doesn't generally provide first-dollar coverage. In other words, the employee isn't able to use the account to pay qualified medical expenses until funds are available in the account for disbursement.

The most significant difference in this healthcare account structure is the opportunity to build equity. With HSAs, every unspent penny accumulates in the employee's account from year to year. Barring any significant health problems, employees who are engaged, responsible for their health, and prudent with their healthcare spending shouldn't spend the full amount allocated to the account every year. Over the course of several years, the money they don't spend on healthcare accumulates in this account and can be used for future qualified healthcare expenses in retirement.

The money in the HSA can be invested just like money in a 401(k) or an Individual Retirement Account (IRA). The account is interest-bearing, and the account owner is not taxed on the interest earned. The withdrawal protocol is also somewhat similar to that of 401(k)s, with one notable exception. If money is withdrawn from the account for qualified medical expenses, the account owner pays no taxes on those disbursements. If account owners use the funds for nonqualified medical expenses, they must pay ordinary income taxes on the amount withdrawn, in addition to a 20% tax penalty. This amounts to approximately a 50% to 60% loss in value. (Note: As this book goes to press, the American Healthcare Act legislation passed by the House of Representatives would change this penalty back to 10%.)

At age 65, you can take penalty-free distributions from the HSA for any reason. However, in order to be both tax-free and penalty-free the distribution must be for a qualified medical expense. Withdrawals made for other purposes will be subject to ordinary income taxes. Since Medicare does not cover all medical expenses, most HSA owners over 65 continue to use their HSA funds for qualified medical expenses.

Somewhat similar to 401(k)s, HSAs have a beneficiary designation and can be transferred from the account owner to his or her spouse tax-free, and those funds will be treated like HSA dollars. If the account owner doesn't have a spouse, the balance in the HSA will be treated like other assets and will be a part of the deceased account owner's estate.

HSA Contribution Strategy

An important consideration for employers is how much HSA funding they'll provide to their employees, and how often they will make a deposit. Employers determine how much they can afford to contribute to employee HSAs and then decide whether lump sum, monthly, quarterly, or annual funding within the annual limit is most appropriate. By working with their employee benefits consultants and health plans, employers can determine the portion of their premium savings that can be reinvested into their employees' HSAs, and then look at their cash flow to determine the ideal frequency of funding.

Employers should consider their employee turnover rate before setting their HSA contribution strategy. Because the HSA is an employee asset, regardless of who funds the account, the money in it is permanent and belongs to that employee. If your employee turnover rate is high, you may want to consider monthly funding to reduce the risk of terminated employees walking away with HSA dollars. Though somewhat more complicated, the IRS permits employers to reverse-discriminate and provide a greater level of funding for lower-paid employees. Regulations followed by the IRS also allow employers to provide a hardship provision, which allows them to advance committed HSA funding to employees who experience a significant health-care event during the year before regularly scheduled HSA contributions are available to them. This provision must be applied uniformly to all employees, and it gives employers added flexibility where and when it's needed most.

The main features of each type of CDHP healthcare account structure are outlined in the table on the following page. Please be aware that this list is not representative of all healthcare account legal provisions, and could be materially impacted by future legislation. Consult your tax advisor for further details.

FSA	HRA	HSA
The Health Dollar Maximizer™	**The Health Dollar Value BuilderTM**	**The Health Dollar Equity BuilderTM**
• Must be used for qualified medical expenses as defined in IRC 213d, including over- the-counter drugs	• Must be used for qualified medical expenses as defined in IRC 213d, including over- the-counter drugs	• May be used for qualified medical expenses as defined in IRC 213d, including over-the-counter drugs
• Use it or lose it	• Use it or keep it—value	• Use it or keep it—equity
• Employee-funded	• Employer-funded	• Employee and/or employer-funded
• Tax-preferred	• Tax-preferred	• Tax-preferred
• Not permanent or portable	• Not permanent or portable	• Permanent and portable
• Earns no interest	• Earns no interest	• Earns interest and balance may be invested with no tax on growth
• No cash-out feature	• No cash-out feature	• Cash-out feature for non-qualified medical expenses (20% penalty) • Note: American Healthcare Act could reduce to 10%
• Funds immediately available	• Funds immediately available	• Funds available when deposited in HSA
• No statutory limits. Employer sets maximum contribution allowed by employee	• No statutory limits. Employer sets maximum contribution	• Treasury Dept. and IRS issue maximum contribution levels
• 3-month grace period is permitted if elected by the employer; rollover up to $500 permitted if employer does not elect a 3-month grace period	• Rollover is discretionary based on employer's plan design	• All funds owned by employee. Monies can be rolled over or transferred at any time to another trustee.
• Employees may forfeit on termination if they don't elect to keep the benefit on COBRA (Consolidated Omnibus Budget Reconciliation Act's continuation of benefits)	• Employees may forfeit on termination if they don't elect to keep the benefit on COBRA (Consolidated Omnibus Budget Reconciliation Act's continuation of benefits)	• Employees may forfeit QHDHP (Qualified High-Deductible Health Plan), but don't forfeit account balances on termination.

The Proof is in the Numbers

As an employer providing health insurance benefits, you're also a client. Once you've weighed the pros and cons of traditional health insurance plans against those of CDHPs, you have a decision to make. If you've decided that you'd like to offer employees the opportunity to participate in CDHPs and improve their physical and financial well-being, you've taken a wonderful first step – the mindset step.

Deciding to offer this opportunity to your employees doesn't have to be an all-or-nothing proposition. In the first year the program is offered, national averages show 5% to 7% of employees will enroll in a CDHP, and this figure is growing as CDHPs become more well-known. As employees gain confidence, more of them will migrate to the CDHP option at open enrollment.

Initially, most people tend to think that CDHPs are meant for the young, healthy, and wealthy, and that they leave older people with health conditions or modest incomes stuck in traditional plans or without insurance of any kind. Numbers from several studies show that this is not at all the case. According to the Employee Benefits Research Institute:

- Enrollment in high-deductible, HSA-eligible health plans is estimated to be between 20–22 million policyholders and their dependents. This compares to 156 million privately insured individuals in the United States in 2015, according to the Kaiser Health Benefits Survey. • 85% of CHDPs currently in place have been opened since the beginning of 2011.

- As of the end of 2015, the average HSA balance was $1,844, up from $1,332 at the beginning of the year. Average account balances increased with the age of the owner of the account. Account balances averaged $759 for owners under age 25 and $3,623 for owners ages 65 and older.

- About 3% of HSAs had invested assets (other than cash). Thirty-six percent of HSAs with invested assets ended 2015 with a balance of $10,000 or more, whereas only 4% of HSAs without invested assets had such a balance. Among HSAs with investments, accounts opened in 2015 ended the year with an average balance of $4,907; those opened in 2005 had an average balance of $27,903 at the end of 2015.

- HSAs with either individual or employer contributions accounted for 59% of all accounts and 78% of total account balances in 2015. Just 3% of these accounts ended the year with a zero balance.

- On average, individuals who made contributions in 2015 contributed $1,864 to their account. HSAs receiving employer contributions in 2015 received $948, on average.

- Four-fifths of HSAs with a 2015 contribution also had a distribution during 2015. Of the HSAs with distributions, the average amount distributed was $1,748.

- Distributions increased as HSA owners' ages increased. For example, 2015 distributions averaged $634 for HSA owners under age 25; they averaged $2,319 for owners ages 55–64; and $2,365 for owners ages 65 and older.

- Distributions were higher for HSAs that were older.

Key Findings

- The number of HSA accounts rose to **20 million, holding almost $37 billion in assets**, a year over year increase of 22% for HSA assets and 20% for accounts for the period between December 31, 2015, and December 31, 2016. HSA accounts now exceed 20 million.

- HSA investments see continued growth. HSA investment assets reached an estimated $5.5 billion in December, up 29% year over year. The average investment account holder has a $14,971 average total balance (deposit and investment account).

- Health plans remain the largest driver of account growth. Health plan partnerships continued as the leading driver of new account growth, accounting for 37% of new accounts opened in 2016.

- Devenir currently projects that by the end of 2018, the HSA market will exceed $50 billion in HSA assets held among more than 27 million accounts.[7]

HSA Assets by Year as of 12/31/16:

Total HSA Assets (in billions)

Year	2006	2007	2008	2009	2010	2011	2012	2013	2014	2015	2016	2017 (est)	2018 (est)
Investments	$.10	$.20	$.20	$.40	$.90	$1.10	$1.75	$2.30	$3.20	$4.20	$5.50	$6.90	$8.80
Deposits	$1.60	$3.20	$5.30	$6.80	$9.0	$11.10	$13.75	$17.10	$21.00	$26.00	$31.50	$37.60	$44.40
Total	$1.7	$3.40	$5.50	$7.20	$9.90	$12.20	$15.50	$19.40	$24.20	$30.20	$37.00	$44.50	$53.20

Source: Devenir Research

These projections demonstrate that the vast majority of consumers could have money rolling over from year to year and could accumulate significant savings over time to help pay for healthcare expenses in future years

The Only Choice

We cannot expect to solve the problems that have led to our national healthcare crisis using the same methods that got us here. By correcting the assumptions, biases, and myths that surround CDHPs, you can help guide employees toward the solution that offers them an alternative to outdated or traditional health insurance options currently available. By providing comprehensive coverage like traditional health plans, the CDHP solution has emerged as not only a viable alternative to managed care but also a pathway to creating a revitalized and sustainable healthcare solution.

Your employees will want an answer to the age-old question: What's in it for me? Now that you know the answer, the following chapters will give you the tools to explain how employees can get more, spend less, save more, and increase their overall health and well-being, all with the support of their employer and their health plan.

Case Study: *Finding the Right Structure*

Janine was the CEO of Bingo Media, a midsized design firm that employed forty-three people. In 2004, she considered switching her employees' health plan to a CDHP. When Janine suggested the switch to her team, the concept of a CDHP appealed to almost everyone. Choosing a CDHP was the easy part. Deciding on a healthcare account structure would present a challenge.

Janine met with the heads of HR and administration to discuss their options. They ruled out FSAs quickly because they didn't like that they were solely employee-funded and that there was little/no potential for rollover. Without these perks, they felt that employees would be less inclined to get involved and make significant lifestyle changes.

Next, they considered HRAs. They liked that these accounts were employer-funded, allowing them to contribute to their employees' health plans, but that they were notional accounts, so the company didn't have to actually pay money until an expense was incurred, which made them feel like it was a less risky proposition. Janine liked the "use it or keep it" aspect of the plan because she wanted her employees motivated to make informed choices.

One year later, renewal time arrived. The implementation and use of the plan had been a success as measured by the low single-digit rate increase they had received, and Janine could tell that people had connected with the system and were making positive changes in their lives. However, she knew there was still room for improvement. After several meetings, it became clear that the main issue holding her employees back was that the money didn't feel like their own. Though the balance of the notional account was rolling over from year to year, people didn't feel like they were saving money and building equity.

When Janine renewed the company's plan, she switched from an HRA to an HSA and noticed the change immediately. Her employees were more proactive in seeking preventive and alternative care, and they made lifestyle changes that improved their health and reduced their reliance on health care. It took a year, but Bingo Media found the plan that worked for them and has been reaping the benefits ever since.

4

A Culture of Health and Wellness

The Root of the Problem

According to the World Health Organization, obesity is now a global epidemic, and North Americans are no small contributors to the growing problem. Around the world, more than 1.6 billion adults are overweight, and of these 400 million qualify as clinically obese. The root causes of this epidemic are the increased consumption of high-calorie foods rich in saturated fats and sugars, coupled with little physical activity.

Being overweight or obese exposes people to diseases that they could avoid by leading healthy and active lifestyles. Type 2 diabetes, cardiovascular disease, hypertension, stroke, and an increased risk of certain types of cancer can all be linked to the extra weight that too many North Americans carry. As the incidence rate of these diseases increases, so does the burden on our healthcare system. A major question arises: how do we turn this disturbing trend around? Many employers are addressing this challenge by making an effort to transform employee behaviors that don't support a healthy lifestyle—and they are starting in the workplace.

It should come as no small surprise that the workplace can have a large effect on an employee's habits. Most people spend at least forty hours per week at their workplace, and when employees are stressed, working in a confined area, and healthy food options aren't available, their health inevitably declines. Clearly, a link exists between work, health, and the healthcare system. As an employer, how do you begin making a change?

Choices, Choices

To address the growing challenge, you, as an employer, have choices to make when you receive an increase in your healthcare spending year after year.

You can do one of the following:

- **Pass the increased premium costs on to your customers by increasing the prices of your products or services.** Are you willing to take the chance that your product or service becomes un-competitively priced and you drive your customers away by doing so?

- **Pass the costs on to your employees by increasing the premium contribution you deduct from their paychecks.** The challenge? Employees appreciate workplace benefits and will be fairly disgruntled to have to pay more for them.

- **Stop offering health insurance to your employees (if federal/state law permits this course of action).** Keep in mind that employees, especially those with families, are drawn to work-places that offer benefits. Failing to provide those benefits might result in many employees looking elsewhere for jobs, and it certainly won't encourage new applicants.

- **Offer a CDHP and build a culture of health and well-being in your workplace that encourages employees and their families to address their own health issues.** Support employees and their families as they improve their overall health and well-being and become less prone to preventable illnesses. The reward? Healthier, more productive employees with fewer claims and lower health plan costs.

Increasing costs and reducing employee benefits isn't going to help anyone. Why not create a company culture of health and wellness that allows you to offer employees even more benefits for working for you? Why not improve overall employee health and well-being and lower health plan costs? If you do, your employees may reap the rewards of a healthier lifestyle, and your business will feel the positive impact of higher productivity and lower health plan costs over time.

Top Cost Drivers

How do you create a culture of health and wellness? A good place to start is by finding out what health problems your employees are most susceptible to. Employee demographics and claims experience reveal that the top five diagnostic categories are typically the same for any organization: cancer, orthopedics, cardiac disease, diabetes, respiratory illness, and behavioral health. The important thing is to identify the major categories that are most manageable and have potential for positive impact by a comprehensive health and wellness program. The following table is an example of the top health risk issues and claim cost drivers a company might have over the course of a year, ranked by cost, from highest to lowest.

ABC Company

2016 Healthcare Management
Renewal Analysis

ABC Company has 1,850 employees. Their Top 10 manageable diseases/conditions are identified below. They are ranked by cost and reflect the most recent months of claims activity.

Disease/Condition Report

Disease/ Condition	Number of claimants with disease	ABC Company prevalence	Health plan prevalence
High cholesterol	214	12.7%	12.3%
High blood pressure	180	10.7%	13.3%
Allergies	85	5.0%	8.5%
Depression	95	5.6%	4.7%
Gastric disease	54	3.2%	3.8%
Low back pain	82	4.9%	5.6%
Heart disease	25	1.5%	2.4%
Chronic renal failure	6	0.4%	0.3%
Diabetes	60	3.6%	4.8%
Peripheral artery disease	7	0.4%	0.4%

- The prevalence rate for the Top 10 manageable diseases and conditions are under or the same as the health plan book of business norms with the exception of depression, which is higher than the health plans' prevalence rates.

- The average age of ABC Company members is thirty-three. The health plan book of business average is 34.1 years of age.

- The largest percentage of the population falls into the 20–44 age segment (37%) with the second largest (32%) in the 45–64 range.

- Given the age distribution of the ABC Company population, it is typical to see utilization related to the top diseases and conditions listed above as well as some cancer and musculo-skeletal disorders.

Most companies with more than one hundred employees can get reports from their health insurance carriers that outline their claims from the previous year, and employers with less than one hundred employees can use company demographics (e.g., age, sex, family size) to predict with reasonable accuracy their overall health risk issues and claim cost drivers. You may have someone in-house who can analyze these reports, or you may want to work with your employee benefits consultant. Identifying your top health risk issues and claim cost drivers will help you understand the most significant health issues plaguing your workforce and driving up your health plan costs.

Armed with this information, your health plan or employee benefits consultant can help you design and implement a worksite wellness program specifically tailored to your health risk issues and claim cost drivers—and you can create a culture of wellness at your company. For example, in our experience, the top seven health-risk behaviors that typically must be addressed are as follows:

1. lack of physical activity,

2. ineffective stress management,

3. poor eating habits,

4. unsuccessful weight management,

5. tobacco use,

6. lack of sleep, and

7. overuse of alcohol.

Every work environment, whether a factory, an office, or a school, should consider building a culture of health and wellness to help employees learn how to live healthier lives. Each of these environments should analyze readily available data to determine the top health risk issues and claim cost drivers. Once you determine your company's health risk issues and claim cost drivers, you can begin tailoring your health and wellness strategy to the unique needs of your workforce.

Personal Health and Its Effect on Health Care

In the context of the previous chapters, the link between personal health and insurance costs may seem obvious, but the cause-and-effect relationship isn't that obvious to employees. When employees don't understand the full cost of medical services, and when their only responsibility within the system is to hand over a standard co-pay as they leave the doctor's office, they don't take the time to consider how their lifestyle choices will affect how much they spend on health care. Once the insurer pays for a service, there's even less reason to be concerned with the cost, and employees aren't likely to be motivated to change poor habits if they aren't held accountable for the factors driving up healthcare spending.

When employees see co-pays replaced with deductibles and coinsurance, and when their expenses are visible and drawn from their healthcare accounts, cost becomes a decidedly more important factor to them. Employees are more inclined to go the extra mile for increased savings when they become educated about how the healthcare system works as a whole, and the ways in which they can reduce their reliance on health services and spend fewer healthcare dollars. But what, exactly, does going that extra mile mean? What can employees do to take the pressure off rising healthcare costs, and how will their efforts help solve the problem? Without this knowledge, all the motivation in the world won't make a difference.

The Foundation

By now you know a CDHP is the combination of an HDHP and a healthcare account, but a CDHP alone won't lower costs and deliver long-term employee behavior changes. The next step is to build a culture of health and wellness. Without a carefully designed employee health and wellness program, your company won't be utilizing one of the major motivating factors that make CDHPs so effective over the long term. One reason that consumers respond so well to CDHPs is the increased feeling of responsibility, flexibility, and control over their health care and money.

Engaging and educating employees is the first step in building a health and wellness culture. Once a consumer sees where every dollar in his or her healthcare account goes, he or she may become motivated to take further steps to change his or her lifestyle and curb healthcare spending. Many employees probably have little idea how their personal health and lifestyle choices affect their healthcare expenses. A good place for them to start is to "know their numbers"—that is, biometric screening data such as blood pressure, cholesterol, and glucose. This means getting a routine physical from a family doctor to establish a baseline of health. If they find that they're unhealthy, they must learn feasible, practical ways to improve their health and well-being.

Only when they understand their individual health challenges and the costs associated with treating those problems will they feel the positive financial implications. This awakening will motivate them to make the changes necessary to decrease health spending and lower health plan costs.

A Likely Story

John works as a plant manager at an engineering firm. It takes him forty-five minutes to get to work from home. He usually leaves for work at 8:00 a.m., stops at a drive-through to grab coffee and a quick greasy breakfast, and is at the office just before 9:00 a.m. A smoker, John has one cigarette before starting his workday. Usually he's bogged down with phone calls, meetings, and e-mail until 1:00 in the afternoon. There aren't many lunch options close to his work, and he doesn't always bring lunch with him, so he drives to a fast-food restaurant ten minutes away, has a cigarette on the way back, and eats lunch at his desk, catching up on e-mails. By the end of the workday, John has had another three cigarettes, and has grabbed two coffees and a candy bar from the snack room, consuming them all at his desk. It's clear that John isn't living a healthy lifestyle. Does he understand the cost and impact of these lifestyle decisions and how easy it might be to change these poor habits?

John's diet and lack of physical activity have the potential to cause a host of problems, including the following:

- diabetes,

- heart disease,

- obesity,

- hypertension (high blood pressure),

- high levels of "bad" (LDL) cholesterol associated with an increased risk of coronary heart disease, and

- stress-related disorders.

John's smoking can also cause a variety of illnesses, including cold symptoms, high blood pressure, impotence, bronchitis, emphysema, stroke, cardiovascular disease, macular degeneration, periodontal disease, and several cancers, including lung cancer.

These lists are by no means exhaustive. John's lifestyle has countless other side effects, some mild, some more severe. Humans are creatures of habit, so without a wake-up call, John could go on indefinitely in his routine. Some subtle changes could make it surprisingly easy for John to make a significant transformation in his health and well-being. If he were to set his alarm fifteen minutes earlier, he would have time to make a more nutritious breakfast at home. Maybe there's a bus that takes him within four blocks of his job; this would add a fifteen-minute walk to the beginning and end of each day. At work, he could take the stairs instead of the elevator, and he could walk over to his colleague's desk to deliver a message instead of calling her extension. Preparing a lunch at night for the next day would help John avoid those calorie-heavy fast-food meals he consumes at lunch; this would eliminate the mid-afternoon energy slumps that lead John to the snack room to grab a coffee and candy bar.

These simple changes would improve John's health and well-being. With education, your employees could achieve the same results. With the addition of worksite wellness programs encouraging healthier eating and incentives to quit smoking, overall employee health and well-being could improve dramatically within a few short months. As an employer, it's your responsibility to educate employees like John, and those with their own unique health concerns, about their health risks, and inspire them to change their lifestyles. For starters, remember that the inspiration for change is different in all of us and that building your culture of wellness takes time and a commitment to education, the cornerstone of a successful wellness program.

Case Study: *Wellness Strategies*

Mary Pratt is the head of an independent private boarding school whose students range in age from fourteen to twenty. Because the senior students are expected to set a good example, they must adhere to the school's strict rules of conduct. Administrators believe that when young people are both learning and living on campus, all members of the school community have a responsibility to keep the campus safe and healthy.

No one understands this more than Mary, who takes her role as head of the school beyond the confines of her office to act as a mentor, role model, and, occasionally, surrogate parent to the school's students. Of course, she expects no less of faculty and staff members. Since adopting a CDHP, the school routinely made its focus on health and wellness clear.

One day, while rounding a corner to enter the school's dining hall, Mary saw several kitchen staff smoking outside the door. A ban on smoking on school property had been built into the rules of conduct, but never had the school considered applying this rule to anyone other than the students. Mary realized that the school had made some tactical errors in its wellness strategy and that the first step to getting back on track was to create a tobacco-free campus.

A tobacco-free campus meant that no one – not students, faculty members, staff, landscapers, cleaners, contractors, vendors, visitors, or service people – could smoke anywhere on school grounds. A wellness committee was formed to develop and oversee the school's approach to a tobacco-free campus, and the committee established some success strategies.

- Tobacco awareness education was available for all faculty, staff, and students.
- The school would sponsor smoking-cessation programs and workshops.
- The school offered guidance and counseling for faculty and staff in need of a nicotine-replacement product on a temporary basis.

One year later, the school is completely tobacco-free, and the entire community has benefited from its positive example.

5

Building a Health and Wellness Program

Building a Culture of Health and Wellness in Your Organization

Even though implementing a health and wellness program can improve your organization's overall performance and lead to increased profitability, you'll still need to convince others of the program's value. How do you get C-level (CEO, CFO) support, and how do you identify financial resources to help offset the investment of implementation?

The workplace is an ideal environment in which to build a culture of health and wellness. Helping your employees adopt healthier lifestyles could have a dramatic effect on your business—50% to 70% of illnesses can be prevented by healthy behavioral changes. Wellness has the potential to boost productivity, driving a three to one return on investment (ROI) over time. CDHP members have a strong financial incentive to participate in health and wellness initiatives. The healthier the individual, the less likely he or she is to incur unnecessary medical expenses. There is a cumulative effect to consider, as well. The Centers for Disease Control and Prevention have stated that wellness is an outcome that is meaningful to not only the individual but to the public as well.

Much has been written about the success in implementing corporate health and wellness programs. In 2014, the Blue Cross Blue Shield Association discovered that CDHP members were more likely to be engaged in wellness initiatives. Based on their internal calculations, the association concluded that:

- 43% participated in health screening (vs. 30% of those in traditional health plans),

- 25% participated in an exercise program (vs. 14% of those in traditional health plans),

- 21% participated in a nutrition/diet program (vs. 15% of those in traditional health plans), and

- 13% used health coaching (vs. 7% of those in traditional health plans).

Making the case for building a culture of health and wellness should include tracking progress (both short-term and long-term results), so you'll always have information to support your pro- gram. How do you measure the success of a health and wellness program? Establish a budget and identify performance expectations to measure your program's effectiveness. Consider your company's vision, financial strength, and strategic priorities so you can explain how building a culture of health and wellness can advance the company's goals. To demonstrate total value, track ROI and routinely share information on performance with all interested parties. Specific data points can include retention, morale, and healthcare cost containment. Determine attainable participation levels for activities and establish increasing goals to maintain involvement as your program matures.

Increasing Chances of Success and Unlocking Financial Resources

Conduct an interest survey and establish a health and wellness committee before launching a program. This will help you gauge interest and find out which initiatives and activities employees are likely to participate in. Consider building a culture of health and wellness in stages. When employers offer too much programming all at once, it usually has trouble getting off the ground; interest and participation wane, and the program is thought to have failed. To ensure this doesn't happen, consider implementing one or two targeted programs in the first year—it's a much more focused and reasonable approach, which can be very successful in terms of interest and participation.

How do you make a business case for financial resources to pay for a health and wellness program? Employing a strategy that helps you fund a health and wellness program with premium contributions from non-compliers is a good place to start. Leveraging your health plan's health and wellness resources is another option. Most health plans offer and support health and wellness programs. Speak to your employee benefits consultant about identifying health and wellness resources, maximizing assistance, and minimizing cost. If you still have doubts about the financial investment required to implement a health and wellness program, consider the long-term benefits. A healthier workforce means fewer sick days, higher productivity, and a happier work environment.

The following graph charts the effects a health and wellness program can have on the amount of money a company spends on health care each year. Programs having a low impact, medium impact, and high impact are compared. These are only the isolated results of a health and wellness program; all the other elements of a CDHP combined with this program will contribute to even greater financial savings.

Healthcare Cost Trend[2]

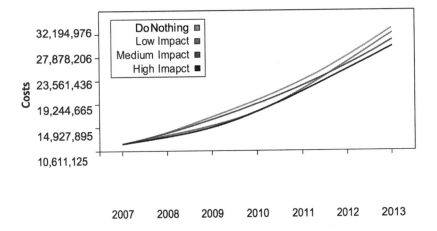

Projected After-Cost Healthcare Savings

Year	Do nothing	Low	Savings	Medium	Savings	High	Savings
Last Year	$ 11,790,139	$ 11,790,139	$ 0	$ 11,790,139	$ 0	$ 11,790,139	$ 0
2008	$ 13,912,364	$ 13,880,564	$ 31,800	$ 13,848,764	$ 63,600	$ 13,816,964	$ 95,400
2009	$ 16,416,590	$ 16,341,542	$ 75,048	$ 16,191,446	$ 225,144	$ 16,078,874	$ 337,716
2010	$ 19,371,576	$ 19,245,495	$ 126,081	$ 18,880,762	$ 490,814	$ 18,597,831	$ 773,745
2011	$ 22,858,459	$ 22,672,160	$ 186,299	$ 22,054,155	$ 804,304	$ 21,570,200	$ 1,288,259
2012	$ 26,972,982	$ 26,715,625	$ 257,357	$ 25,798,759	$ 1,174,223	$ 25,002,548	$ 1,970,434
2013	$ 31,828,119	$ 31,486,913	$ 341,205	$ 30,217,391	$ 1,610,727	$ 28,940,147	$ 2,887,972

(Source: WellSteps, LLC www.wellsteps.com)

The graph clearly indicates that the money you invest in a health and wellness program will be more than returned by the results. You'll have a healthier, more productive workforce, and you'll spend less on health care.

Health and Wellness Program Development

Building a culture of health and wellness begins with asking some philosophical questions about your company:

1. When it comes to employee benefits, does your organization tend to make decisions on behalf of employees or do you encourage employees to get involved in making their own decisions?

2. Would you describe your company as innovative and risk-taking, or more conservative and risk-averse?

3. What are your general impressions about employee lifestyle choices? Is your workforce generally healthy already or are there significant health challenges—such as widespread smoking—that need to be addressed?

4. Are wellness values shared across your organization?

5. Does your leadership team lead by example?

6. Is employee health a top priority for everyone?

7. Does your company provide a positive and supportive peer environment?

8. Do you as a company do things that make it easy for employees to adopt and maintain a healthy lifestyle?

The answers to these questions will guide you in developing your health and wellness strategy, and help you decide which type of health and wellness program is best suited to your organization. Health and wellness programs take many shapes and forms—and they tend to fall into one of two categories: encouragement based or performance based.

Encouragement-Based Health and Wellness Programs

In an encouragement-based health and wellness program, rewards and incentives are created to motivate plan members to participate in health and wellness activities. Rewards or incentives are earned when the plan members participate in the program but are not tied to the outcomes of those activities.

The following are examples of rewards in encouragement-based health and wellness programs:

- Employees are offered flexible work schedules to participate in weight-loss programs.

- Plan members are awarded reduced gym membership fees.

- Plan members are given free flu shots for themselves and their family members.

- Smokers are fully reimbursed (or partially reimbursed) for tobacco replacement products.

There are no rules when creating encouragement-based health and wellness programs, except that they must be available to all similarly situated individuals (i.e., available to all and subject to nondiscrimination rules and regulations). The challenge with this model is that different levels of interventions or program impact are not addressed.

Performance-Based Health and Wellness Programs

In a performance-based health and wellness program, any rewards or penalties associated with the program are linked to an individual's ability to meet clearly defined performance standards related to a specific health metric. For example, employees may be rewarded for reaching a healthy body weight or body mass index (BMI), lowering their cholesterol, or quitting smoking.

The Department of Labor sets the criteria for a performance-based health and wellness program, which are summarized below.[8] Be sure to consult the most current regulations to ensure full compliance.

1. The program must be reasonably designed to promote health and prevent disease.

2. The program and its rewards must be available to all similarly situated individuals. There must also be a reasonable measurement alternative available.

3. The program must disclose the availability of a reasonable measurement alternative in all program materials. The employer may ask a plan member to provide a doctor's note that verifies the need for an alternative measurement, and a doctor's suggestion of what measurement would be appropriate. Most employers will need the assistance of a clinician to evaluate claims for alternative measurement standards, as well as to avoid having to view confidential health information, minimizing Health Insurance Portability and Accountability Act (HIPAA) privacy issues.

4. Individuals who are eligible to participate must be given a chance to qualify at least once per year.

5. The amount of the reward offered by the program cannot exceed 50% of the applicable cost of coverage.

So, where do you begin? Start by implementing a CDHP and an encouragement-based approach to health and wellness. In this first phase, you reward plan members for "knowing their numbers" (e.g., blood pressure, cholesterol, glucose, body mass index). The following year, you could adopt a performance-based approach to health and wellness by offering employees the ability to earn rewards for reaching certain targets or by participating in health education, exercise plans, or other programs designed to improve overall health and well-being. In year three and beyond, consider making the incentives available only for plan members reaching cer- tain targets, with alternative measurements available where legally required.

This phased-in approach to building a culture of health and well-being will give your employees time to get comfortable with the new culture, and take steps to improve their health and well-being before they experience a financial (or personal) consequence.

Best Practices for Health and Wellness Program Management

The Wellness Council of America (WELCOA), an organization dedicated to the promotion of worksite wellness, has identified the seven best practices (the Seven Cs) for employers to follow when building a comprehensive, effective worksite wellness program within their organizations. (For more information on WELCOA, please visit www.welcoa.org.)

The Seven Cs

1. **Capture senior-level support**

   A commitment from the top is critical to the success of any wellness initiative. Management must understand the benefits of the program for both the employees and the organization and be willing to put funds toward its development, implementation, and evaluation. Descriptions of what competitors are doing in the way of health promotion and linking health promotion to business goals, values, and strategic priorities will help secure senior management support. Managers who take part in the program have a better chance of influencing others to participate.

2. Create a wellness team

Wellness teams should include a cross-section of potential program participants, including employees. Your team should include individuals who will have a role in program development, implementation, and evaluation. This ensures broad ownership of the program and more innovative ideas. A wellness team will help garner buy-in from both management and participants, develop a program that is responsive to the needs of all potential participants, and will be responsible for overseeing all of the company's wellness efforts.

3. Collect data that will drive your health initiatives

Once your team is in place and management is on board, gather baseline data to help assess employee health interests and risks. The results of your data collection will guide you in what kind of health programs to offer. This process may involve a survey of employee interest in various health initiatives, health risk assessments, and claims analysis to determine current employee disease risk.

4. Craft an annual operating plan

For your wellness program to succeed, you must have a plan. An annual operating plan should include a mission statement for the program along with specific, measurable short- and long-term goals and objectives. Your program is more likely to succeed if it is linked to the company's strategic initiatives, as it will have a better chance of maintaining management's support throughout implementation. A written plan also provides continuity when members of the wellness committee change and is instrumental in holding the team accountable to the goals, objectives, and timeline agreed upon.

5. Choose appropriate health initiatives

The health initiatives you choose should come from your data (e.g., survey, HRA aggregate report, claims). The data should address prevailing risk factors in your employee population and be in line with what both management and employees want from the wellness program.

6. Create a supportive environment

A supportive environment provides employees with encouragement, opportunity, and rewards. A culture of health that supports worksite health promotion might have such features as healthy food choices in vending machines, a no-smoking policy, and flexible work schedules that allow workers to exercise. Celebrate and reward health achievements and have a management team that models healthy behavior. Most importantly, a culture of health involves employees in every aspect of the wellness program from design and promotion, to implementation and evaluation.

7. Consistently evaluate your outcomes

Evaluation involves taking a close look at your goals and objectives and determining whether you achieved your desired result. Evaluation allows you to celebrate goals that have been achieved and to discontinue or change ineffective initiatives.

Case Study: *Bending the Trend through Engagement, Education, Incentives, and Rewards*

With approximately 850 employees, Woodard & Curran is one of the leading environmental engineering consulting firms in the United States. The company's leaders are passionate about supporting the employees that make their company successful. They believe that traditional health insurance benefits, while essential, are not enough. Their mission statement begins with a promise to their employees to create a great place to work by offering comprehensive benefits.

Woodard & Curran was an early adopter of the CDHP solution. With more than a decade of experience in offering CDHP, they found the right strategy for their company was to offer their employees a choice of two health insurance plans. The first option was a CDHP paired with a health savings account. This option was selected by 75% of their employees. The structure: Woodard & Curran covers a portion of the plan deductible by funding an HSA for its employees and their families. The funding schedule is tiered based on income, providing higher HSA contributions to lower paid employees and phasing out any contribution for highly paid employees ($90k+). The second option available to employees was a more expensive non-qualified high-deductible health plan featuring 80%/60% coinsurance for in- and out-of-network healthcare, respectively.

Woodard's management team put in place a successful healthcare strategy by leveraging the power of a CDHP/HSA and encouraging employees to set aside additional pretax money to save for their own medical expenses. When employees contribute their own HSA monies through payroll, they avoid federal and state taxes—and both the employee and the employer save on FICA taxes.

Management wanted to do even more. The company put in place a thoughtful long-term strategy to help its employees become healthier and to support them in making better lifestyle choices. This strategy was hugely successful, in large measure because it received strong support from the CEO all the way down through the organization.

Woodard & Curran established a wellness committee that was tasked with meeting each month. Each company location designated a wellness champion to take part in those monthly meetings, report on the progress of key initiatives, and interact with other employees about a wide range of health and well-being initiatives.

In the beginning, the wellness initiatives focused heavily on education and encouraging people to take part in simple exercise programs. They started with a basic walking initiative and quickly engaged employees with internal friendly competitions. This approach led to greater engagement among staff and improved morale, supporting the company's vision of employee health and well-being as a priority. Over the years, the company intensified and broadened its commitment to this strategy, transforming the culture of the organization in a profound and sustainable way.

With an eye on continued expansion of their wellness program, Woodard & Curran recently introduced a new online health and well-being portal, Virgin Pulse, which monitors activity, gathers critical data, and points members toward specific solutions that are appropriate to their situation. In the first two weeks after Virgin Portal was introduced, 55% of employees had enrolled in it—a remarkably high figure demonstrating the strong engagement of Woodard & Curran employees.

Using this portal, each location can now perform targeted challenges and schedule site-specific activities that support long-term health and well-being. The portal also incorporates a variety of reward programs to encourage and reward the right behaviors. Employees taking part in certain activities can earn points over time and receive cash rewards, which are paid into their HSA account or through payroll. As another part of its long-term well-being strategy, Woodard & Curran established a fitness center in the corporate office and brought in trainers to work with employees.

A sense of shared commitment to employee health has made the company's CDHP/HSA strategy a huge financial and health success—and a major strategic advantage when it comes to retaining and recruiting key employees. At Woodard & Curran, employee health and well-being is not merely a priority, but one of the company's core values.

6

Evolving from Wellness to Well-Being

We've all had the experience of feeling like information is coming at us from a bewildering array of sources. At times, this experience becomes information overload, and the stressful feeling of having too much data to process in too little time can be intensified by any number of other factors: the government may be more present in our businesses than it was in the past; our competitors may be highly astute and may move rapidly, requiring us to move just as quickly; and the exponential creation and adoption of new technologies may change the ways in which we work and live on a daily basis. As if all that weren't enough, our home- and work-life demands are, in all likelihood, challenging and rigorous. In short, the world in which we live is filled with pressure, stress, and plenty of causes for anxiety. Most of us are experiencing more disruptive change than ever before. Every day, our world is becoming more complex and moving faster—and whether we realize it or not, employee stress can be a significant business challenge. Rest assured: when your employees are stressed, your clients and customers will notice!

This state of affairs does not signify doom and gloom. Instead, it spells opportunity to make a difference.

Albert Einstein once observed that the world, as we have created it, is a product of our own thinking. It cannot be changed unless our thinking is changed. In this chapter, we propose a change in thinking that can help us make sense of the challenging modern environment in which we live—the evolution from wellness to well-being.

Well-Being: A Sustainable, High-Impact Approach

Traditionally, people think of wellness, and more specifically wellness programs when they think of healthcare plans. Wellness is generally understood to mean the adoption of healthy lifestyle habits, physical activity, and a healthy diet. We tend to view wellness as a linear process that moves people through various programs, perhaps resulting in a reward when they complete certain activities. This wellness focus is largely tactical. It's short term in nature, and it's often led by a third party outside of our organizations.

Well-being, on the other hand, is an organizational transformation that embraces a whole-person approach and moves beyond superficial behavioral changes suggested by an outsider.

Well-being reflects a commitment to continuous improvement for the individual and the entire organization. A strategy focused on well-being helps you to take a long-term view of everything that happens in the workplace. It helps the executive team to be more committed to the health and viability of the organization—and its most valuable asset, the employees.

Wellness is a one-off, program-sponsored focus. Well-being offers a very different approach, namely the transformation of your organization's entire culture toward a mind-set of continuous improvement and personal accountability, including, but not limited to, all aspects of individual health.

For a well-being focus to make a difference, for it to stick in a way that provides forward momentum for your organization and everyone in it, you must make well-being a core component of the corporate strategy. It must be understood and embraced at all levels of the organization, from the top down.

Yes, this takes effort and commitment. But when it happens, well-being has a far greater positive impact, and is much more sustainable than any wellness program. This is because well-being addresses employee issues holistically rather than in a linear manner. It affects everything you do, from the creation of a healthy eating and exercise routine to the forging of strong social relationships, from presenteeism in the workplace to the fulfillment of critical long-term goals. Where wellness is impersonal, disengaged, and transitional, a powerful culture built around well-being is personal, meaningful, and enduring.

The Five Elements of Health and Well-Being

The five elements of health and well-being are: (1) physical, (2) financial, (3) workplace, (4) community, and (5) mind and spirit. These five elements are interconnected, and are viewed as the fundamental factors when creating, reinforcing, and sustaining a culture of health and well-being for the long term. They must be the focus of ongoing, active effort. If you skip or minimize the importance of taking action in any one of the five areas, your culture is missing an integral part of the well-being equation.

Let's take a closer look at each of these elements.

1. **Physical well-being**

   Physical well-being means having good health and enough energy to do the tasks that are expected of you on a daily basis. Not everyone has the same level of physical health, but everyone can move toward the goal of living life at an optimum state of health and vibrancy. Failing to deal effectively with physical stressors undermines personal (and, by extension, organizational) well-being.

2. **Financial well-being**

   Financial well-being is the ability to manage your personal finances and feel secure with the freedom to choose how you want to enjoy life. Often, an employee who is facing major financial stress will end up with health issues, and that lowers not only her own well-being, but also the organization's well-being.

3. **Workplace well-being**

   Workplace well-being means being supported as you develop both personally and professionally, so that you are more engaged in your work on a daily basis. A member of the team who is not engaged creates distraction that negatively impacts productivity. In turn, this negative impact lowers the standard of workplace well-being for the organization as a whole.

4. **Community Well-being**

   Community well-being is about giving back to the communities that you and your business serve. The motto of the American Red Cross is "giving is good for the donor and the recipient." It's about living an attitude of gratitude. Providing an opportunity for your employees to participate in activities that help your community has a profound impact on morale and spirit, both for the individual and the organization.

5. **Mind and Spirit**

   Mind and spirit is about helping you become centered, to balance yourself, and to reflect and contemplate your future direction and vision. This element is all about being fully present in the moment, about mindfulness, a critical attribute for everyone in the organization, and an essential cultural attribute in successful teams.

Creating a Culture of Well-Being

To create a culture of well-being in your organization, you will need to adopt the following six-step process.

Step One: Engagement

The creation of a culture of health and well-being will go nowhere unless there is ownership and senior-level support for an engaged and healthy culture. It is essential to start with an internal committee that focuses regularly on the status of the organization's ongoing well-being initiatives. This committee should be staffed with people who are passionate about a well-being culture and represent all levels of the organization. Engaging this group will demonstrate to the organization as a whole your desire to evolve—and create commitment at all levels.

Step Two: Cultural Environment

Assess your current cultural environment. Are you providing opportunities for people to work out during the day? Are you offering vending machines or other resources that have healthy food and drink options? Are there opportunities for people to share in high-quality healthy food together? Are there group activities? Is there some active campaign to give back to the community? Are there opportunities for private time and suggestions on how to sustain mindfulness even when things get hectic?

Step Three: A Multiyear Health and Well-Being Strategy

Develop a multiyear health and well-being strategy. This kind of strategy will help you set short-, mid-, and long-term goals in each of the five areas, and address and create the culture of well-being. Create clear benchmarks and milestones for success along your journey.

Step Four: Infuse Vision

A culture of health and well-being needs to become the new cultural norm in your organization. It should not be viewed as a one-off program. The best way to infuse this vision is by constant, varied communication from people at the top of the organization. Note that this is not a one-time speech or initiative, but an ongoing responsibility of senior management to articulate the vision for well-being, and to live that vision.

Step Five: Lifestyle and Behavior

Implement and focus on specific, sustainable changes to people's lifestyles and behavior. Create and support action-oriented programs that engage and modify behavior. An example is to provide resources for a weight management, stress management, smoking cessation, or an exercise program.

Step Six: Evaluation

Examine the milestones and track the results of employees' engagement in a well-being program. Evaluate what is working well, what is not working well, and what needs to be changed. Celebrate when your team or specific employees achieve certain milestones!

Measuring the Success of Your Well-Being Strategy

To determine the effectiveness of your well-being strategy, consider answering the following questions:

- Has there been an improvement in education, knowledge, attitudes, and behaviors of your employees in each of the five areas of well-being?

- Have your employees embraced your well-being initiatives?

- How many employees are participating in your program?

- What type of feedback are you receiving from your employees?

- Have you seen an overall improvement in employee engagement in the workplace?

- What specific areas affecting well-being have been addressed through your corporate strategy?

- What specific actions have been undertaken in support of well-being in each area?

- If you offer health insurance in your workplace, how has your health plan actually performed? What specific impacts has it had? Has it impacted your health plan utilization? Use objective, quantitative, and qualitative measures to assess whether this strategy is having a positive impact on the physical well-being of your employee population in each area.

Measuring the overall success of your efforts to build and foster a culture of health and well-being can be a challenge, one that demands a nuanced approach. An effective strategy is one that continually supports new and innovative ways to keep your employees engaged and thinking differently about their own personal journeys and the impact on your organization.

Well-Being: The Competitive Edge

It takes talent, passion, and teamwork to compete in today's highly competitive, highly stressful work environment. Creating and sustaining a corporate well-being strategy starts with culture, leadership, and communication. It is an intelligent investment in your organization's ability to compete and thrive in today's environment. Investing in your people is the very best way to grow your business, and having a culture that embraces well-being at its core provides a unique competitive advantage that will attract and retain human capital—your business's most precious asset.

Case Study: *Lifestyle and Behavior Changes Lead to Reduction in Unnecessary Medical Procedures, and Higher Quality of Life*

Cheverus High School is a private, Jesuit, college-preparatory school founded in 1917, in Portland, Maine. With more than 425 students and 145 faculty and staff, the school is dedicated to fostering intellectual, spiritual, physical, and personal excellence.

After years of double-digit health insurance rate increases, it was time for Cheverus High School to find a better alternative. The school leadership spent two years carefully studying the Captivated Health solution and in 2015, the Cheverus board decided to leave the fully insured market and strategically collaborate with other schools in a partially self-insured health insurance captive program called Captivated Health®. One of the key factors behind the school's decision was its desire to bend the trend on its annual fully insured rate increases—a virtually impossible feat in a fully insured marketplace, especially where the school did not have access to data, hampering efforts to be proactive. By participating in the Captivated Health® program, the school aimed to achieve long-term stability and predictability.

An integral part of the Captivated Health® solution is to create a culture of well-being that goes beyond routine medical care and delves into the physical, financial, workplace, community, and mind/spirit areas. This approach, which takes a holistic view of each employee and the employee's family, leads to greater employee productivity as well as improved health outcomes.

Cheverus worked with Captivated's dedicated health and well-being team to craft a multiyear strategy that would engage and educate employees. Once employees understand that today's claims are tomorrow's premiums, they behave differently and make more informed choices. Consistent with Cheverus's desire to engage and support its faculty and staff, the school created business partnerships with nutritionists, personal health coaches, and a local fitness center to offer advice and guidance at no cost to the faculty, staff, and their families.

continued

A wonderful example of a positive outcome of this strategy and the forward-thinking approach by the school was when a faculty member's spouse was advised that he needed gastric bypass surgery to deal with an obesity problem. This type of surgery costs, on average, approximately $100,000. Before he committed to the surgery, the spouse worked with a nutritionist who had a business partnership with the school. The nutritionist took the time to understand the challenges facing the spouse and offered personalized advice and guidance. By following this advice, the spouse managed to change his lifestyle and lose the necessary weight—and to avoid unnecessary surgery. Not only did this represent a better financial outcome for the school and the Captivated Health ® program, it had a positive, life-changing impact on both the employee and her spouse.

7

Implementation and Communication

Introducing the CDHP Solution

If your organization is considering adopting a CDHP, your employees' curiosity has probably been piqued by a swirl of rumors. They've probably heard that they could spend less on health care, become healthier, and even save for the future. Along with the good rumors, though, bad ones are sure to spread. They may have heard that they'll spend more on health care with these types of health insurance plans, seek less preventive care, and forgo necessary medical care because they won't want to spend the money in their healthcare accounts. It takes a careful and well-planned communication and implementation plan to educate employees about the responsibilities and positive aspects of CDHPs, as well as the best ways to avoid the potential pitfalls. Change is difficult, and most people resist a transition even when it's beneficial—so don't be surprised if there is some initial hesitation.

It's your job to facilitate a plan that will help everyone at your organization become comfortable with the principles, mechanics, and language of CDHPs. This chapter will explain how to design an effective, personalized communication and education plan to introduce employees to the responsibilities and benefits of a CDHP. It will help you engage, educate, and empower them as consumers of health care.

Support Systems

Getting the right people involved in the communication and education process is important. As an employer, it's your decision to offer a CDHP, but you can't take on the responsibility of single-handedly educating your workforce. A successful CDHP implementation starts with leadership commitment and active support of the plan. What follows is a support system for employees during the transition. In the early stages, there must be a system in place for them to ask questions, access materials, and receive coaching.

Start by meeting with your employee benefits consultant, HR department, management team, and insurance carrier. Based on their feedback, which might include their particular areas of interest, you can begin delegating responsibilities. Your employee benefits consultant and insurance carrier can work together to organize initial enrollment meetings. You might ask in-house staff to form an employee benefits committee to gather employee feedback and ensure that all members are getting help with their first couple of claims and associated paperwork. Follow-up services, such as one-on-one consultations, can be offered later.

Strong communication and education plans encourage the successful adoption of CDHPs:

1. **Education.** Preliminary education meetings and focus groups will ensure that all employees have a basic understanding of the philosophy and mechanics of CDHPs relative to traditional managed-care plans. Without these meetings, terms and concepts referred to in the literature will be foreign, and employees may become overwhelmed. Introducing users to the basics gives them a chance to become familiar with the material before they have to make any decisions.

2. **Support.** Only so much information can be absorbed at once, so employees are bound to have further questions after the initial educational meetings. Having an informed and supportive employee benefits consultant as well as in-house personnel trained to discuss concerns and provide further resources encourages employees to ask questions. You don't want employees to give up out of frustration and decide to stay with their old plan. If people can pop into a co-worker's

office and get the information they need, they're more likely to follow up on their questions and concerns, and to feel more comfortable with the change in plans.

3. **Ongoing communication.** Learning how to be a healthcare consumer takes time, and it only becomes real to your employees when they make a claim. Expect more questions when they start to use the CDHP, receive EOBs, and have to pay their providers for the care they receive. Anticipate member anxiety and confusion by building ongoing communications into your plans. Employees and their families will need it, and your proactive approach will be well received.

Focus on the Foundation: The Three Principles of CDHPs

Facilitators will communicate the plan's philosophy of transparency, responsibility, and opportunity to employees as well as what the plan covers and how. In every communication, focus on the direct impact these principles will have on employees. Keep the points outlined in the following front and center in all your communications and education meetings. Staying on message is critical to successful implementation because it helps your employees speak the same language.

Transparency

- **Awareness.** The first step toward becoming knowledgeable on any subject is accepting that you may not have all of the information. It's no accident that consumers don't know how much health services cost. Insurers and providers keep them in the dark because their contracts prohibit full disclosure of how and what insurers are paid. Let employees know that they've been in the dark about health care. When they realize that important information hasn't been shared with them, they'll start asking questions that most insurers and physicians aren't used to answering. Your employees will want to understand their alternatives. You can inform them that the CDHP solution creates awareness, and that the plan encourages the full disclosure of all treatment options, costs, and fees.

- **Information.** Once employees are aware of gaps in their knowledge, they'll want to know more about healthcare costs and how their personal situations can be better managed. The EOB, which an employee will receive from his or her insurance company, is the document that will help the employee better understand the cost of healthcare services and verify the services received. Tell your employees that the EOB will not only detail the costs of their healthcare expenses but also break down each expense into its individual components, illustrating how much money goes to hospitals, doctors, and pharmacies. Members won't have to make a special request to access this information—it's an integral step in the healthcare process with a CDHP. An EOB will be issued for each medical service they access, so they'll always know the full and discounted cost of their care.

Responsibility

- **Increasing knowledge.** With knowledge comes responsibility. When employees understand that they have the power of choice, they can take time to review their options and make more informed decisions. Reading the EOB carefully and understanding what it says is one way consumers can inform themselves about their personal medical expenses. Individuals can be more engaged in their healthcare choices in many ways and take steps to change how they live their lives and interact with the healthcare system.

- **Resources.** Cost-comparative tools can be trustworthy sources, such as federal and state healthcare cost websites. Many health insurance companies offer nurse help lines, a valuable resource for employees that will save them time and money. Nurses can provide much of the same information and knowledge a doctor would, but the telephone service normally costs employees nothing because carriers offer it as a value-added benefit. Telemedicine is also making inroads by offering consumers the opportunity to seek medical care (primary care, behavioral health, and nutrition counseling) from the comfort of their own homes. This form of healthcare is usually less than $100 per visit, substantially less expensive than pursuing other more traditional options. It's crucial to the plan's success that employees learn how to improve their personal health and rely less on health services,; resources of the kind we're discussing may encourage them to change negative habits. These simple tools are probably news to most people, so build awareness of them into your communication plan.

- **Considering alternatives.** Encourage employees to choose less expensive medical care when possible. Someone with a broken arm should go to the hospital, but someone who knows he has only twisted his ankle may want to ice it for a day or two, keep it elevated, and try to stay off his feet. If the ankle is still sore and swollen after a few days, he would likely see a doctor, but it's important to take alternative measures first. These measures could possibly save a few hundred dollars that it would cost to have a doctor give the same advice, or to fill a prescription for a painkiller when an over-the-counter drug would suffice. Healthcare cost and quality depend on where you live, who you are, and what's known about your condition and will factor into your decision-making process.

- **Improving health and wellness.** Learning how your health directly affects your healthcare spending can be a major wake-up call. Employees should be encouraged to think about how they can improve their health through diet, exercise, and stress management. Health improvement plans that are determined for them won't work. They must decide where their health needs the most improvement, and what sorts of initiatives will inspire them to make meaningful changes.

Opportunity

- **Reducing healthcare costs and saving money.** This is a major benefit of CDHPs and should be highlighted throughout the communication and education process. Employees can use their healthcare accounts as a vehicle for the tax-favored payment of healthcare services. The more they live by the CDHP philosophy, the more value or equity they can build in their CDHP. By becoming informed, taking advantage of alternative approaches for minor health issues (e.g., speaking to a health nurse, or taking advantage of telemedicine), and staying in good physical shape, they're more likely to have value or equity left over at the end of each year, which rolls over and builds over time.

This built-in incentive creates a significant financial opportunity for CDHP members.

- **Becoming healthier.** Aside from the financial benefits of improving one's health, there are also obvious health benefits. By taking advantage of this unique value proposition, employees can change their lifestyles and become healthier, stronger, and more productive in every area of their lives.

- **Contributing to the greater good.** Though it's compelling to think about the personal advantages of CDHPs, it's important to remind employees about the big picture. CDHPs are a solution that helps consumers personally reduce one of the biggest expenses every employer has (usually second only after payroll), which can be a real threat to most organizations' financial health.

Implementation

Your communication plan has to start at the top. Organizational leadership should be educated early, and the communication plan should include your HR personnel and management team. Once you've firmly established support at the higher levels of your organization, you can begin introducing employees to this solution. You want to build enthusiasm among your management and HR teams, and get most of them on board before offering the plan to the rest of the company. Employees are more likely to react positively to a new health plan when they see there's already support for it—support lends the plan legitimacy.

Organizational Leadership

Enthusiasm for the CDHP needs to trickle down from the top, so the first people to engage, educate, and empower are those at the most senior level. Senior leaders should be educated about the principles and mechanics of CDHPs so that they're able to instill understanding and enthusiasm in those they'll be communicating with. When management is introduced to the CDHP solution, the senior leaders' enthusiasm will inspire them to support and champion the program.

An informed and excited senior leadership team means enthusiastic managers, which means enthusiastic employees. If senior leaders aren't excited about the plan, why would anyone else be? Start at the top, and by the time the information has reached your employees, they'll embrace the CDHP solution.

Human Resources

Your human resources team is critical to successfully implementing the plan. They must feel comfortable with their understanding of the CDHP. Getting them on board early by working with your employee benefits consultant and insurance provider can set the tone for the entire transition. Having invested years in the previous plan's administration, HR personnel must be convinced that it's worth the initial effort of switching from a traditional managed-care plan to a CDHP. Once HR is convinced, they could be your most ardent supporters.

Initially, HR may see the CDHP solution as a lot more work and the education challenges more daunting. As the plan administrators and the liaison to your employees, HR must have the most complete understanding of CDHPs. You must not underestimate their influence on your staff. If HR is confused and unconvinced that these changes are for the best, employees will hesitate to even consider a new health plan offering. When your HR team is informed and confident, their attitude will help employees feel much more comfortable with the change.

Mandatory Management Meetings and Employee Education

Most employees have a more casual approach to getting information and will go to their managers when they have concerns. Managers must be able to handle questions and discuss the responsibilities and advantages of CDHPs when approached for advice. Their comfort level and vocal support are critical to successfully implementing these plans.

Mandatory management meetings serve to educate management and coach them on passing their knowledge on to employees. Managers will be able to address many concerns directly, but it's a good idea to have HR prepare a package for managers that includes a list of helpful websites like CDHPCoach.com, pamphlets or guidebooks, and other resources. If managers can't resolve employees' questions themselves, they can consult additional resources. If they still don't have answers, they can always refer employees to HR, who should be glad to help. In turn, HR should be able to lean on your employee benefits consultant for hands-on assistance and support.

Once senior leaders, management, and HR are on board, it's time to introduce your employees to CDHPs. Because consumers tend to stick to what they know and are comfortable with, you have to ensure that employees are exposed to meaningful information about CDHPs and absorb it. Sending out a communication or a brochure isn't enough. Few people will actually read it, and printed information isn't particularly persuasive these days. It's hard to imagine anyone becoming convinced to make a change this big based on a few bullet points, especially if there's no one around to address their concerns and questions. Mandatory employee education sessions will ensure that employees are exposed to information about CDHPs in a dynamic and effective way.

Face-to-face communication is the most effective way to get employees engaged and excited about a new product. In a group environment, they can ask the seminar leader questions as they come up, and everyone in the group benefits from the answers. Once employees become familiar with the basics, they can weigh the advantages and disadvantages of CDHPs against those of their current health plan. This will enable employees to make a decision that's more informed than simply choosing the option they know over the one they don't. The benefit to the employer is that educating all employees at once saves both time and money, and increases the probability that they will choose the CDHP solution.

Communication and Education

Every company should have a communication and education strategy tailored specifically to its unique needs. Understand who your target audience is: Who makes up the majority of your staff? Consider your employees' average age, education level, and family size to determine what sort of approach might work best for most of them, but also incorporate options for individual learning and communication styles. By pairing a master strategy geared to your general audience with special options for the needs of individuals, you ensure that no employee is left behind.

When sharing information, keep it simple and be frank. Don't try to cover everything at once—the first step is to explain the reasons for adopting a CDHP. Describe these reasons and provide specific examples to illustrate why CDHPs make sense for most employers and your company. Start by explaining the company's unique health risk issues. What challenges and risk issues are your employees facing as a general population, and what health issues do they risk developing because of workplace and lifestyle habits? Use summary reports from your carrier or employee benefits consultant to support this information. Illustrate where health dollars are being consistently spent, and explain the factors that have been driving up health insurance premiums.

Provide examples of hypothetical consumers who suffer from the top three health challenges prevalent in your employee population, and compare their out-of-pocket healthcare expenses as CDHP members to those of traditional health plan subscribers with the same health issues. It's the most effective way to portray similarities and differences between the CDHP solution and traditional health insurance plans. Keep it simple, make it real, and, wherever possible, make it personal.

Use Examples

Until employees firmly grasp how CDHPs work, it's almost impossible to have too many examples. Create scenarios that employees can relate to. Use real-life examples of people accessing the healthcare system and incurring claims so they can see how the healthcare transaction process works and how to use their healthcare accounts and health insurance plan to pay for their medical expenses.

To be as effective as possible, the examples should include details about how much typical procedures cost and how they're billed, the process for payment, and how these costs affect the money in the consumer's healthcare account. Examples might illustrate how accounts are created for employees, how contributions are made to those accounts, and how much value or equity might roll over in a typical year. The more varied the examples, the more people will relate to them, so include examples of people and families with different healthcare conditions, expenses, and funds available for use. You can ask your employee benefits consultant and health plan for assistance with these educational tools.

Use Simple Language

You want to avoid overwhelming or confusing your employees, because there's no quicker way to turn people off a new product than to frustrate them. If it seems like too much work to under- stand the CDHP solution, no one will want to make the effort to switch to the new health plan. Ensure that the facilitator of your educational meetings uses accessible language to explain new terms or difficult concepts, and doesn't assume that employees know the basics about health insurance, let alone CDHPs. If your facilitator casually uses unfamiliar terms and acronyms, people will leave the meeting more confused than when they came in. Using straightforward language to discuss CDHPs will make the whole solution more helpful and appealing.

Offer Various Media

Everyone absorbs information differently, so it's important to present employees with a variety of media to help them learn about CDHPs. Face-to-face communication has been proven to be the most effective way to disperse information, but your communication strategy shouldn't end there. Some people have trouble processing information as quickly as it comes in a meeting, so they might need resources to take away with them. Others like to conduct their own research, and others might want to take even more material home to show their families. Videos from online sources such as YouTube and relevant case studies are important tools to consider as well.

To cater to individual needs, a variety of communication methods is encouraged.

- **Face-to-face.** Personal communication is central to CDHP education, and this part of the communication plan should never be overlooked. Employees can ask for clarification, examples, or further information and get immediate results.

- **Print.** Brochures, pamphlets, and guidebooks compiled from helpful printouts can be effective. Your employees will use them to remind themselves of any details they might have forgotten during the meeting, and can take them home to share with partners and families.

- **Websites/Mobile Applications.** Defining terms with the click of a mouse and following links to other online resources can be useful when learning about a new subject. Ask your facilitator to recommend a few helpful websites and mobile apps that you can share with employees (www.hsainsider.com or www.cdhpcoach.com).

- **Webinars.** Many people learn more effectively from electronic media. They like to pause when they want, look things up when they're lost, and access material from anywhere. A narrated slide presentation can be effective for people with this learning style. If you have access to a webinar presentation from your employee benefits consultant or your insurer, make it available to employees.

Before you select the media you'll use for your employee education meetings, survey your employees about their preferred type of media so your employee benefits consultant or insurer can cater to their preferences. Consumers usually like to have independent access to information before making big decisions, so the ability to visit an Internet resource or peruse a folder of helpful printouts might be the difference between reluctant and convinced employees.

Seek Feedback

You can't effectively tailor a program for your staff if you don't know what they want, so throughout the education process, ask which aspects of the communication and education program are working for them and which aren't. Be consistent with the CDHP philosophy and encourage employee involvement and independent decision-making. Ask them to provide feedback to you, your employee benefits consultant, and your insurer on ways to improve communication and education.

Don't be discouraged if your employees aren't immediately excited about the CDHP. It may take time. People who have used a particular health insurance plan for most of their lives aren't likely to abandon it overnight. Be prepared to face initial skepticism and a lot of questions before employees come to trust the CDHP solution. View it as an opportunity to provide additional information that will remove their doubts and help them transition in a positive way.

Compare and Contrast Plans

Though the main purpose of the educational meetings is to inform employees about CDHPs, it's also a good idea to ensure employees fully understand their current health insurance plan. With most traditional health insurance plans, decision-making power is in the hands of doctors or insurance companies, and, over time, members get used to the co-pay structure without really knowing how the transaction side of healthcare works. Without knowledge of plan mechanics, how can employees compare their current health insurance plan to a CDHP?

The first step is to clarify how traditional managed-care plans work, how much services cost on average, how co-pays shield them from the actual cost of care, and why health insurance premiums are rising faster than overall inflation. Ensure that your staff understands that sustained health insurance premium increases will cause them and your company to pay higher premiums and have less control over where their healthcare dollars are spent. Once they understand the facts, introduce them to the tools that will help them compare plans. These should be explained in simple terms, with the help of examples. Equipped with this knowledge and these tools, employees will be able to compare all aspects of CDHPs to those of their current plan.

Provide Post-Meeting Resources

The educational process doesn't end when the meetings are over. Questions will occur to people after the meetings, particularly as they incur their first claims. To provide employees the support they'll need, it will be important to have continued access to CDHP resources and extra printed and online materials available at your workplace.

Again, nothing takes the place of face-to-face communication. There should be someone on-site to answer any questions during the employee research and evaluation process. Ideally, this should be a member of your HR team, someone with whom your employees are familiar and comfortable, and someone who's passionate about the transition to a CDHP.

To supplement the personal touch, technology can also assist you. One application that is helpful is CDHPCoach.com. It's an online resource for all things CDHP for the employer and helpful to the consumer. It's easy to navigate and a free place to learn the language of CDHP. Online tools like this can help establish a baseline of knowledge for CDHP use and assist employers, employees, and their family members to build their healthcare confidence.

Case Study: *Taking the Message to the People in a Personal Way Maximizes Enrollment*

Cimpress, the parent company of Vistaprint, is an international producer of customizable marketing materials, signage, and other products employing over 10,000 people worldwide. In 2013, the company offered four health plan options for US employees. The plan options offered had no deductibles or very low deductibles and were designed primarily with co-payments for healthcare services. The company financed their health plan on a fully insured basis for its 1,000 US-based employees and had favorable claims experiences, which is why they did not see a compelling reason to change to a CDHP.

In consultation with its employee benefits advisor, Cimpress learned more about current healthcare market trends and the potential negative impact on the company's health insurance plan. Cimpress's management team realized that its current healthcare strategy was unsustainable. They decided to adopt the "fix the roof before it's raining" mind-set and embraced the migration to a CDHP paired with a health savings account (HSA). Cimpress's leadership understood that future premium increases were inevitable due to rising healthcare costs and became aware of the importance of looking beyond short-term cost challenges and committed to developing a long-term strategy that would support changes in employee lifestyle and behavior. These changes, management believed, would help employees and their families take charge of their own health and well-being, as well as start to see the true cost of healthcare—and result in better employee health and reduced costs for Cimpress and employees over time.

In April 2015, Cimpress' introduced the CDHP/HSA option at open enrollment and set about the long task of educating employees and their families on lifestyle choices and personal behavior and their impact on overall health. This strategy involved people at all levels of the organization, and relied heavily on personal support from senior leadership and the benefits team. Such engagement was critical, because the plan would only be successful if it was actively supported by company leadership.

continued

Cimpress eliminated health plan options with no deductibles and offered the employees the choice of staying on the health plans with low deductibles and paying a higher percentage of the monthly premium, or enrolling in the lower cost CDHP/HSA where Cimpress would fund half the deductible through an HSA. Providing a choice was an important part of the implementation, as Cimpress did not want employees to feel they were forced to select a CDHP. The company agreed to fund the HSA on a semiannual basis.

Long before beginning open enrollment for the new CDHP/HSA, the benefits advisor initiated a comprehensive targeted communication strategy to inform Cimpress employees of the advantages and unique benefits of the new CDHP/HSA over the traditional health plan alternatives. The advisor also covered the various processes involved, and answered specific questions about how the plan worked.

This educational initiative relied heavily on face-to-face discussions with Cimpress employees, using webinars only as backup if employees couldn't make the open enrollment meetings. At these in-person meetings, employees received comprehensive answers to their questions, along with plenty of educational resources. In this way, the benefits advisor's team was able to take into account the varied learning styles of the people involved. As a result, employees were deeply engaged in the discussion and excited about the new plan.

In a strategy meeting with human resources leadership prior to open enrollment, the advisor shared that if Cimpress's leadership followed the best practices for implementation outlined in this book, the initial take-up rate for the CDHP would be 26%. This estimate was far greater than the 10% predicted by some members of the Cimpress team, as they initially assumed it would take a longer amount of time to educate employees on a CDHP. They were relying on prior work experience and past financial modeling used to calculate the total potential cost impact. A friendly gentleman's bet on the final outcome was sealed with a handshake and all parties worked collaboratively for a great result.

Management agreed to a comprehensive implementation plan, and the advisor continued to use the power of in-person communication and on-site meetings to move beyond questions about deductibles and the HSA into a deeper discussion about the long-term impact on health and how to lower costs without sacrificing quality. When open enrollment concluded, the take-up rate for the CDHP/HSA was 26%—exactly the figure the advisor had predicted!

Once the CDHP/HSA was operational, regularly scheduled on-site meetings continued, as they were seen as the key to successful implementation. After a few months of being on the plan, to further the learning a series of in-depth post-enrollment conversations with employees and their families addressed the inevitable questions and concerns about the new plan. This time the learning focused on practical application. The meetings reinforced everything that had been covered in the pre-enrollment and enrollment periods, revisiting as necessary information on such issues as how to use the HSA and how to file and be reimbursed for deductible eligible claims.

The continuous education and communication approach strengthened the sense of partnership that now existed between Cimpress management and employees in addressing individual healthcare issues. As a direct result of that partnership, the enrollment in the CDHP/HSA increased to 37% in 2016 and a remarkable 44% in 2017, saving millions of premium dollars for the company and its employees and their families. Cimpress's strategic move to the CDHP/HSA is a case study in success by following the best practices outlined in this book. That success has been due in a large measure to the firm's exemplary education and implementation plan and the commitment of their leadership team.

8

Education
Best Practices

Learning the Mechanics

Breaking down the CDHP components and processes into manageable parts will help order the information and prevent the meeting facilitator from teaching too much too fast. When discussing the CDHP mechanics portion of the education plan with facilitators, consider the following breakdown as a guide to organizing the material.

Types of CDHPs

Employees must be aware of the differences between the healthcare account structures your company may offer: FSAs, HRAs, and HSAs. If you offer employees a choice of CDHP healthcare account structures, take time to explain the benefits and differences of each account so they can understand which account structure works best for them. As a diverse population, your employees have different healthcare needs and different ways of managing their money. The features and benefits that will make one person favor an HRA may be unappealing to someone who prefers the features and benefits of an HSA.

Distribute a printout or provide a link to your intranet/benefits administration platform that highlights each plan's primary features to illustrate their differences. Another way to acquaint employees with the different kinds of CDHPs and how they compare to traditional plans is to demonstrate a typical year of medical expenses. For example, if, in one year, Jasmine has one physical, fills four prescriptions, and makes six visits to her physical therapist, what will her spending be when her healthcare account is an FSA, an HRA, or an HSA? What will her complete financial picture (premium and cost sharing) be with each? Will she have rollover funds at the end of the year? Will she incur out-of-pocket (OOP) costs? What will her premium savings total? Compare the answers to these questions to the results she would see if she were on a traditional managed-care plan. The table that follows is a compelling way to present these findings.

Purchasing Power of a $750 HRA

Procedure	Member Cost	Healthcare Account	CDHP OOP	HMO OOP
1 Pap Smear	$15	$15	$0	$0
1 Annual Exam	$120	$0	$0	$20
5 Physical Therapy Visits	$350	$350	$0	$100
3 Prescriptions	$138	$0	$60	$60
1 Physician Office Visit/Consult	$60	$60	$0	$20
Total	**$683**	**$425**	**$60**	**$200**
HRA Rollover		**$325**		

Purchasing Power of a $1,500 HRA

Procedure	Member Cost	Healthcare Account	CDHP OOP	HMO OOP
4 Allergy Tests	$20	$20	$0	$0
6 Childhood Immunizations	$90	$90	$0	$0
6 Prescriptions	$276	$0	$120	$120
4 Physician Office Visits/Consults	$240	$240	$0	$80
1 Outpatient Surgery Visit	$750	$750	$0	$500
1 Emergency Room Visit	$500	$400	$100	$150
2 Well-Child Exams	$160	$0	$0	$40
Total	**$2036**	**$1500**	**$220**	**$890**
HRA Rollover		**$0**		

People who are just beginning to learn about CDHPs may be unfamiliar with healthcare account structures. Most health insurance members are familiar with paying a higher premium for their health plan in exchange for smaller co-pays and out-of-pocket expenses for healthcare services as they access them. So, when you introduce employees to the idea of being responsible for managing their own healthcare accounts, expect to see some interesting reactions—this is new to them. By maintaining a structured communication and education plan, you'll have your employees speaking the CDHP language in no time.

Using Your Account

Employees will learn that visiting the doctor and incurring claims will be slightly different than it was under their old plan. For starters, there's more administrative work for them to manage when using a healthcare account. Explain the basic process of using medical services, receiving bills from their providers and EOBs from their health plan, understanding these communication tools, and making payments for healthcare services. Different accounts use different methods of payment, including paper claim form filing, debit cards, direct deposit, and checks, but the essential process remains the same.

Healthcare Account Flowchart

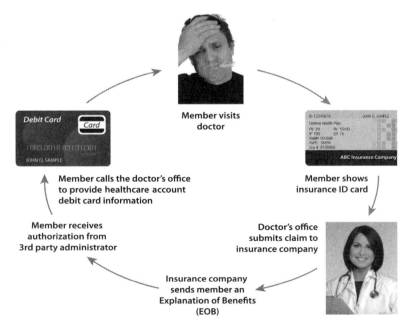

Member visits doctor

Member shows insurance ID card

Member calls the doctor's office to provide healthcare account debit card information

Doctor's office submits claim to insurance company

Member receives authorization from 3rd party administrator

Insurance company sends member an Explanation of Benefits (EOB)

Each time CDHP members go to the doctor, they should present the medical ID card they receive from their health plan. In most cases, they will not be required to pay for the service on the spot, as they would with most traditional health plans. Instead, their doctors will submit their bills to their health insurance companies for processing. The insurers will adjudicate their claims and send the members EOBs that tell them how much they owe. At this point, members call their doctors' offices and pay their bills directly with checks or healthcare account debit cards, or they file paper claims for reimbursement.

Depending on the structure of their plan, members may be required to pay a discounted rate for prescription drugs they purchase at the pharmacy. For example, if they're enrolled in a QHDHP and haven't met their annual deductible, they're required to pay for the medication at the pharmacy. In this case, they should pay with their debit cards and keep their receipts to either give to their healthcare account administrator or retain for record-keeping purposes, in case they are ever audited by the Internal Revenue Service (IRS).

Though these processes all sound simple, when employees are familiar with paying a co-pay at their doctor's office and then walking away, receiving EOBs for their expenses might come as a surprise. Work with your employee benefits consultant and healthcare account administrator to show examples of the different paperwork and email communications they'll receive every time they access the healthcare system.

To reinforce what new members have learned, offer plenty of examples. You might illustrate the steps various hypothetical CDHP members take when they access health services—how Judy pays her bill after seeing her doctor for a physical, what Dimitri does when he refills his prescription, and what Rosa does when she takes her daughter to the emergency room with a broken arm. Seeing the process repeated will increase your employees' comfort level, and their fear of the unknown won't deter them from choosing a CDHP. The education won't stick until they incur their first claim; however, providing illustrations gives them context and eases the transition from theory to practice.

The following points offer a few helpful hints for employees to be aware of when they use their CDHPs.

Key points to remember when using a CDHP built with a QHDHP:

- Present your medical ID card every time you access medical services or products. Without it, you'll pay retail when you're entitled to wholesale prices, which are negotiated by your health insurance carrier.

- Never pay for medical services at the doctor's office (unless this has been pre-arranged), even if the receptionist asks that you do so. If your doctor participates in your health plan, chances are he or she has a contract with your insurance company that requires you to be given a pre-negotiated discount. The discount will be calculated through your insurer when the claim is adjudicated, and you will not be balance billed.

- Pay for medical services after you receive your EOB from your health insurance company. You're paying the amount indicated on your EOB, not your doctor's bill, and there may be significant differences between the two.

- You may be asked to pay the discounted price of a drug at the pharmacy. In this case, pay with your healthcare account's debit card if available or submit the bill to your healthcare account administrator for reimbursement after you pay out-of-pocket.

- This information should prepare employees for the first few times they use their new healthcare accounts. Remember, there will be many questions in the early stages of CDHP adoption, which is why it's important to provide follow-up help and ongoing communication.

Financial Savings

Your employees are likely to find the financial savings to be one of the CDHP's most appealing aspects, but it's also one that might cause some skepticism. The prospect of saving money is always attractive, but it often gives rise to suspicion if it sounds too good to be true. The earlier examples comparing the yearly healthcare expenses of CDHP members to those of traditional health plan members help make your case: CDHPs can save you money if you live a healthy lifestyle and make more informed purchasing choices when you access the healthcare system. Having a little bit of luck and good genetics doesn't hurt, either.

After your employees have reviewed these examples, demonstrate the rollover capabilities of these funds, not just over the course of a year, but over the course of their working lives. Saving several hundred dollars a year sounds nice, but rolling over unused funds from year to year, eliminating out-of-pocket costs, and retiring with a substantial sum of money in the bank if you have an HSA sounds even better. To help employees visualize the accumulation, mock up a typical user's healthcare expenses over a period of several years to show the accumulation of funds over both good years and challenging ones.

Though these examples cover the potential financial savings, remind employees that CDHP membership has further financial benefits. For example, funds deposited in HSAs are not subject to income tax, grow tax-free with interest or gains from mutual funds, and remain untaxed if withdrawn for medical expenses. At any age, members can withdraw money from their accounts for any reason. If those withdrawals are before age sixty-five and are not for qualified medical expenses, they're subject to penalties and income tax, at their current tax rate. After age 65 and in retirement years, the savings accumulated in an HSA account can be significant.

According to Hong Kong and Shanghai Banking Corporation's annual retirement survey, 76% of Americans see the cost of health care as the largest barrier to saving for retirement; 61% consider illness in a partner as a close second.

Healthcare Costs for Seniors

Healthcare expenses during retirement years increase substantially because of increased longevity.

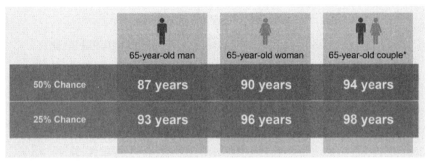

(Source: Society of Actuaries RP-2014 Mortality Table projected with Mortality Improvement Scale MP-2014 as of 2015. For illustrative purposes.)

Healthcare expenses during retirement years increase substantially because of increased longevity. Health care after retirement is more expensive than most people realize.

The average sixty-five-year-old couple who retired in 2015 with Medicare insurance coverage will needed an average of $276,000 to cover medical expenses during the combined remainder of their lifetimes. This estimate includes deductibles, supplemental insurance premiums, out-of-pocket expenses, and services excluded by Medicare. The figure does not include over-the-counter medications, most dental services, and most long-term care expenses—and will be a good deal higher if they need to use a nursing home. (Traditional Medicare [Part A] covers inpatient hospital costs and stays in skilled nursing facilities plus hospice care.)

No matter what the motivating factor is for the employee to engage in an HSA, it is important to emphasize that the power to preserve and save is in their hands. It's true that certain people, for various reasons, are more prone to illness than others, but preventive measures can often make a world of difference. Every good decision users make, whether it's going for a jog, eating a healthy diet, or buckling their seatbelts, has the potential to save them money. Positive behavior changes add up to substantial savings over time.

Spreading Accountability

Knowing that the consumer must be responsible isn't enough to change employees' lifestyles. The first step is teaching them how to be responsible. Inspiring employees to improve their health is a major part of the CDHP philosophy, so effectively communicate this to them.

Employees with unhealthy lifestyles may not be thinking about the future. They may not be feeling the effects of their choices now, so educate them on what consuming a high-fat diet means for their long-term health. Explain how neglecting physical exercise in their thirties affects their muscle mass and bone density in their fifties. Teach them why a high-stress lifestyle could result in a heart attack, and help them put their health into perspective so they see its enormous effect on both their finances and their quality of life.

Improving health and well-being is the most important step toward reducing reliance on health care. Even healthy people get sick or hurt from time to time, and steps can be taken to make these unavoidable events less damaging financially. The following scenarios illustrate some ineffective ways to handle medical situations, and suggest more effective choices and outcomes.

Situation 1

You develop an earache over the weekend, and your doctor's office is closed. You decide to go to the emergency room, where you wait more than four hours to be seen by a doctor. The cost could run over $900.

A better choice: This isn't an emergency, so a trip to a walk-in clinic or urgent care facility may be more appropriate. The wait won't be as long, and it will cost around $120. Or you can take advantage of telemedicine in the privacy of your own home for something in the neighborhood of $50.

Situation 2

You wake up in the morning with a runny nose and sore throat. You make an appointment with your doctor and sit for half an hour in the waiting room before seeing him. Treating your head cold costs you around $150.

A better choice: Call/text your direct primary care doctor and describe your symptoms. Pick up the over-the-counter medication she will probably recommend, and pay less than $10.

Situation 3

While biking without a helmet, you get cut off by a car and suffer a nasty fall that results in a concussion. An ambulance is called and you're rushed to the hospital, where they treat your concussion and keep you there overnight for observation. The bill is $13,000.

A better choice: Wear a helmet. You may have suffered some cuts and bruises in the fall from your bike, but your injuries wouldn't be life-threatening. You could have avoided incurring the expense of an ambulance, and fixing cuts and scrapes cost much less than treating a skull fracture.

The lesson to be taken from these scenarios is that the CDHP philosophy doesn't discourage healthcare use at any cost. Sometimes significant financial costs can't be avoided, and that's what health insurance is designed to cover—the unexpected. However, exercising caution, seeking preventive care, and making smart decisions can avoid many small and large costs, resulting in increased personal savings. If your organization is large enough (usually over one hundred employees) to be renewed based on your claims experience (also known as experience rating), you should expect lower renewal costs.

Summing It All Up

Understanding CDHPs is a lot of information to digest, so devote the final stages of your communication and education plan to an overview of what was discussed in previous education meetings, leaving plenty of time at the end for questions. The information that employees have learned over the course of the communication and education process should be fresh in their minds when it comes time to make a decision. Assure your staff that if any questions occur to them in the coming days or weeks, there will be resources available to them, and request a commitment for those resources from your employee benefits consulting firm, health plan, and healthcare account administration partners. Employees should leave feeling comfortable with the subject matter and aware of the support system that has been put in place should they need it.

Highlight the following points in the final stages:

- **Be engaged.** Take control of your purchasing power, and exercise your options when it comes to accessing health care. Learn how to live a healthier and more responsible lifestyle so you can avoid accessing the healthcare system for unnecessary products or services.

- **Be informed.** Learn everything you can about CDHPs from your employee benefits consultant and health plan partners. Resources and coaching should be available, so take advan- tage of it. The goal of CDHP members is to be informed. Consider the plan that's best for you, how much money you'll potentially save, and how much your health will improve. If you stumble over any of these issues, ask for help.

- **Be proactive.** Why feel sick and pay for medical services when you can prevent illness? Everyone can improve personal habits to save money and improve their quality of life, such as deciding to wear a seatbelt, exercise, or eat a healthy diet.

- **Be discerning.** Empower yourself with education, and act like a consumer. Healthcare consumers shouldn't buy or settle for the first thing they're offered; they should investigate their options. Call a health plan nurse help line if you have a minor ailment, and ask if there's a generic alternative available when your doctor writes you a prescription. Alternatively, you can check this online at GoodRx.com. The idea isn't to cut corners, but to get the best value for your money.

- **Be smart with your money.** Why give your money away when you can keep it? Because the consumer funds the FSA and the HSA, not only do you save your money, but when you take advantage of these healthcare accounts, you don't pay taxes on the money you deposit, and you lower the financial impact of out-of-pocket healthcare expenses by using those tax-preferred dollars to pay for qualified medical expenses. With the HSA, it's not a risky investment because the premium savings generated by the QHDHP can be deposited in your HSA, and the insurance plan covers you if your healthcare spending exceeds your deductible. Save your money on a tax-preferred basis, earn tax-free interest with an HSA, and be in control of how you spend your savings.

This innovative solution to rising healthcare costs is so loaded with consumer benefits that it's hard to imagine your employees won't find it compelling. As an employer, you want employees to spend less, know more, save money, and become healthier. Implementing this long-term solution in your workplace will help change their interactions with the healthcare system and allow them to live a healthier and more responsible lifestyle. Doesn't that sound refreshing in today's challenging times?

Using the communication and education best practices outlined in this chapter will ensure that employees have a comfortable learning environment and are never overwhelmed by too much information or confused by health insurance and financial jargon. By the end of the communication and education phase of implementation, employees should be confident in their knowledge of healthcare terminology, CDHP philosophy, and mechanics, and they should be excited by the prospect of potential financial returns. Don't be surprised if many are eager to trade in their traditional health insurance plan right away. In fact, when open enrollment comes to a close, they'll know more about CDHPs than they do about the health plans they've been using for decades.

Case Study: *Communication Is Key*

After years of overwhelming choices and confusing plan designs, a major consortium of private schools in the Northeast pooled its schools together to purchase group health insurance for all members. As soon as the group came together, each member school individually met with Karen, an employee benefits consultant who carefully explained how a CDHP would be an effective way for the schools to engage faculty and staff in their healthcare choices and save their schools and faculty and staff money on health insurance premiums.

At a time when the member schools were straining to operate within their budgets, it was a well-received message that their schools and members would pay less for a CDHP and receive the same quality of health care that they'd been receiving under their managed-care plan. After reviewing the information Karen provided, the leaders of the schools in the consortium agreed that, if properly managed, the CDHP she had proposed would engage their faculty and staff in taking control of their healthcare choices. It would also save the schools and faculty and staff money and translate into manageable renewal increases over time.

continued

Convinced of the CDHP's value, the group's task was to offer faculty and staff at each school the same level of thoughtful education they'd received from the employee benefits consultant. The schools made a three-year shift of membership into the CDHP, and took time educating faculty and staff on how the CDHP would work and how it would benefit them, both as individuals and as a group.

For the first few years, faculty and staff at member schools were offered both a traditional managed-care plan and a CDHP. Karen helped to set up and execute a thoughtful communication and education plan and took the time to answer the group's questions as they worked out the details of the plan.

When each school's administration team first met with faculty and staff to discuss the CDHP, they found that many of them had trouble grasping the concept. They understood everything was still covered under their health plan, but the mechanics of how the plan worked was different and somewhat confusing, like most new things. Karen and a representative from the insurance provider were at the introductory meetings as well as the head of school and senior leadership to demonstrate the importance of this change and to help educate faculty and staff. There was also time set aside in each of the schools to address their private concerns and answer any questions directly.

For most schools the initial education phase took a week and was done during the school day and reinforced in faculty and staff meetings. The amount of time invested proved to be quite valuable as each person needed to fully understand the changes in the school's new health insurance program. There were many advantages in the school's decision to move to the CDHP and that message was important for all faculty and staff to hear. To help faculty and staff with the timing difference of HSA deposits by the schools and when their members incurred medical claims subject to their deductible, most of the schools implemented a hardship provision, which would advance the school's contribution to a member's HSA should a need for healthcare funds arise before the school was scheduled to make a deposit. This provided the faculty and staff with assurances that they would not be financially burdened during the process of building up their HSAs. It was one of the many ways the schools were able to address these types of concerns during the strategic planning phase.

An individualized approach to communication and education helps boost CDHP enrollment. In the first year, the consortium successfully enrolled 26% of its eligible faculty and staff into the CDHP—far outstripping the national average of 6%.

It is human nature to resist what we don't understand. The less confusing the health insurance plan, the more appealing it becomes. As the group of private schools story suggests, an employee benefits consultant like Karen who truly understands the CDHP solution, an enthusiastic administration team, and an insurance provider willing to support the communication and education plan are all invaluable to a smooth transition from a managed-care plan to a CDHP.

9

Post-Implementation Communication and Education

Early Stages

Once open enrollment closes, the employer's focus changes from introducing the CDHP to continually developing employee awareness of their health status and interaction with both the healthcare system and their health plan. Education will remain part of ongoing communication efforts, but your approach to communication and education will shift to addressing issues that arise as employees use their CDHP and incur claims, and later, as their needs change, to reinforcing the CDHP's value.

As discussed in the previous chapter, using a variety of learning tools, such as face-to-face communication, printed materials, and electronic resources such as company intranets, benefits administration systems, and education portals like CDHPCoach.com, will help you ensure that all users benefit from the information, no matter what their learning styles are. Continue to use varied learning tools as you move into this next phase. It's vital to the learning process and overall success of the CDHP solution.

Reinforcement
A Helpful Resource

No matter how successful your education meetings are and how well your employees receive their new health plan, expect a learning curve. Often, time will pass between when employees learn about the mechanics of the CDHP and when they incur their first health claim. If they take the CDHP philosophy to heart and make intelligent use of resources such as nurse help lines, they may not actually need to use their CDHP for weeks or months, and hopefully even longer. By the time a consumer incurs a claim, the how-to lesson will no longer be fresh in his or her mind.

You've already provided your employees with resources to which they can refer when struggling with a CDHP-related process, but you might also ask your employee benefits consultant and HR team to compile well-organized instructions with information on using the plan. Examples include when to use the debit card or file a paper-based reimbursement form, how to read the EOB, and what documents to send to the insurance provider or TPA for pro- cessing. Instructions can be distributed to each CDHP member, and all members need to do is check the information guide's billing section before heading to the doctor's office. Ideally, the information guide will answer most questions.

Helpful tools such as these should be made available by your health plan, TPA, or employee benefits consultant. They are inexpensive to assemble, are easy to use, and last indefinitely, as sections can always be updated with new information. A member of your HR team should be the primary contact for your employee benefits consultant, TPA, and health plan. Your employee benefits consultant and insurer should inform this person when procedures change or new rules are introduced. Revised sections can be printed and dis- tributed to all CDHP members at the company, and members can remove the old section and insert the updated version. Information can be kept up to date without having to replace the entire resource every year or two, which can be costly.

No matter how comprehensive the information guide is, it can't answer every question that will arise as members use their CDHP. This is why face-to-face communication continues to be so important, even after the switch to CDHPs. Aside from answering questions, further education meetings enhance and maintain a knowledge base for CDHP processes and teach employees how to become smarter healthcare consumers over time.

Member Education Forums

Once CDHPs have been implemented, and especially during the first year of use, you'll want to conduct member education forums to develop employee knowledge of healthcare terminology, plan mechanics, and administrative processes.

To determine where employees need the most guidance, administer a survey using an electronic survey tool after the first round of educational meetings, and ask which areas need more explanation. Make these areas your first priority, then conduct another survey a few months after implementation and ask the same question. Undoubtedly, as the scope of plan use expands, new concerns will arise. Employee comfort with the CDHP remains important after implementation, so continue to identify problem areas and organize education forums to address the specific issues troubling employees.

Terminology

A frequent stumbling block for new CDHP members is learning a whole new set of terminology. There are dozens of acronyms to keep in mind, and it can be challenging to remember the difference between an HRA and an HSA, or a CDHP and an HDHP. Even a common term such as *preventive healthcare* may seem intimidating to someone who has no idea what it means. By defining the term (e.g., measures people can take before they get sick to decrease the odds of illness) and offering a few examples (e.g., immunizations and a healthy diet), you can guarantee that when the term is used in an education meeting or in any CDHP-related context, your employees will be clear on its meaning and comfortable using it.

If your employees are having trouble keeping terminology straight, chances are they're also having trouble understanding what those terms mean. One way to handle this is to provide resources devoted to demystifying healthcare terminology. The resources will ensure that employees become familiar and comfortable with all the new terms they need to understand to make their own healthcare decisions. You can also distribute a glossary to help employees learn terms faster, and they'll always be able to look something up if they don't understand it on tools like CDHPCoach.com. See if your employee benefits consultant, insurer, or TPA can provide a glossary, or ask HR to create one.

Plan Mechanics

Some employees may not be maximizing their benefits because they're unaware of the resources and value. If, for example, after three months of CDHP use, two-thirds of employees report hav- ing difficulty grasping the cost breakdowns on their EOBs, you'll know you need to address that learn- ing issue so it won't negatively affect the CDHP's successful adoption.

Find out which bits and pieces of the mechanical process might be caus- ing problems for employees, and hold focused education forums on these top- ics. If you find that certain employees are particularly knowledgeable about specific topics—perhaps billing, preventive healthcare options, or wellness— name them as go-to people for other staff members with questions related to their area of expertise. Just as various information sources—printed, elec- tronic, face-to-face—cater to people with different learning styles, having a peer to consult, as well as a formal educational atmosphere, allows employees to gather information comfortably.

Administrative Processes

Your employees don't have to be as familiar with CDHP administrative pro- cesses as your HR team will be, but they should have some idea of what goes on behind the scenes. HR-led information sessions are a cost-effective way to introduce employees to a part of CDHP mechanics that they may never otherwise understand. If employees know who to talk to when they have healthcare account management issues, they'll seek that help and not feel lost.

On the other hand, if employees don't know who to go to when they have problems managing their healthcare accounts, they'll get frustrated, and the negative experience will damage their satisfaction with the CDHP. Clearly defining the roles of administrative personnel and who can help with specific issues will prevent this confusion and lost productivity.

Turning Theory into Application

Much of the post-implementation effort is geared toward helping employees and their families use the information and resources they've learned in prac- tice. Reference resources are a great help, but let's review some exercises that can benefit the shift from classroom lessons to real-life application.

Real-Life Claiming Examples

Using an anecdotal tone to offer real-life examples of CDHP claiming can help employees relate to what they're learning. It's important to teach them how to manage their healthcare accounts when they incur a claim and where the money goes once they've paid their bills. However, there's a big difference between understanding the theoretical process and going through the actual process by yourself, especially during times of poor health.

After you've explained the technical part of managing the healthcare account, employees should see examples of real people making real claims. Replace a standard flowchart with a real person so they can put themselves in the person's shoes. Here's an example:

> Joe has a history of high blood pressure and wakes up one morning to find his heart racing. He calls his doctor and arranges an appointment for that morning. At his doctor's office, Joe presents his medical ID card. His doctor discovers that Joe's medicine isn't strong enough and prescribes a newer, more potent medication. At Joe's request, the doctor recommends a generic variety that will reduce his costs.
>
> Joe checks out at reception, making sure his doctor's office will send the bill to his insurer, and heads to the pharmacy. At the pharmacy, Joe is charged $43.56 for his prescription medication, and he uses his HSA debit card to pay for it and keeps the receipt for his tax records.
>
> Joe goes home, takes his medication, and files his prescription drug receipt with his tax records. A week later, Joe receives an EOB in the mail, detailing the costs of his doctor's visit. After reading over the EOB, Joe calls his doctor's office and provides his HSA MasterCard or VISA information, and his account is debited for his office visit.

Employees will relate to Joe's experience and understand the simple steps he takes to access medical care and how to pay for it.

To cover as many bases as possible, use real-life claim examples for various services, such as annual checkups, buying prescription drugs, regular physical therapy appointments, emergency room visits, and trips to the walk-in clinic.

Sharing Experiences and Responsibility

To ease the transition from theory to practice, ask employees if they are willing to share their experiences with their CDHP. If they've had challenges, other members may be able to offer advice based on their own experiences, and members who have had a few opportunities to use their CDHP can offer strategies to simplify the process. Discussing challenges and strategies with peers not only helps employees solve problems but also creates a sense of community and provides them with another helpful resource—each other—to access when they have questions.

Your employees should understand their role as members and your role as a sponsor and facilitator of a CDHP. Responsibility is an important motivator in the CDHP solution, and it should be clear that everyone at the company has a role to play. After all, they're all participating in the improvement of both fiscal and physical wellness. The principle of shared responsibility is an important element to reinforce with your employees.

Healthcare Account Management

There are three types of healthcare accounts—FSAs, HRAs, and HSAs—and each requires a different level of responsibility and administrative management. The following pages explain the kinds of administrative processes required for each healthcare account.

Flexible Spending Accounts

Employees

Flexible spending accounts operate according to IRS Section 125 regulations, and are used for the tax-preferred reimbursement of qualified medical expenses as defined by Section 213(d) of the IRS code. On average, using this tax-preferred healthcare account to pay for expenses can lower out-of-pocket medical expenses for employees by as much as 33%, depending on their tax bracket.

When an employee enrolls in an FSA, it's for the entire plan year (determined by the employer). During enrollment, employees determine the dollar amount they want to contribute to the FSA, which isn't to exceed the maximum set by the employer, and that annual amount is divided by the number of payroll periods in the plan year and deducted each pay period. During the plan year, employees access these tax-preferred funds with a debit card or file paper claims. Employees may change their contribution amount within sixty days of a qualified status change (e.g., marriage, divorce, death). Should an employee have a positive balance in his or her FSA at the end of the plan year, that amount will be forfeited back to the employer and used to offset plan administrative costs.

By law, during the plan year, the employee must provide proof of purchase to the FSA administrator to verify that the funds were spent on qualified medical expenses. The frequency of receipt verification shouldn't overburden employees because it will occur most frequently as a result of a purchase made at a pharmacy or grocery store rather than the doctor's office. Most merchants (e.g., CVS, Walgreens, Rite Aid) are now equipped with the Inventory Information Approval System, which verifies qualified medical expenses paid for by the FSA debit card. Employees should retain their receipts in case they're audited.

If an employee terminates employment during the plan year, deductions will stop at the point of employment termination. Coverage for qualifying expenses ends at the date of the last payroll deduction. The FSA is a COBRA (Consolidated Omnibus Budget Reconciliation Act) eligible benefit and can be elected by the employee when he or she terminates employment, though it must be funded with after-tax dollars. In either event, this provision is particularly helpful to the employee so he or she won't leave a positive balance in the FSA.

Employers

FSAs help an employer lower employees' taxable income and save FICA, unemployment insurance, workers' compensation, and other wage-based benefits. An employer will save 7.65% in FICA taxes on every dollar.

Because the FSA is a salary reduction plan, the employer needs a Section 125 plan document to establish the plan and allow employees to deduct their FSA contributions on a tax-preferred basis. Once employees have made their annual elections, the employer will divide those elections by the number of payroll periods in their plan year and deduct the appropriate amounts each pay period. In turn, the employer deposits those funds in a separate account or forwards them to the FSA administrator.

Administration of the FSA is usually delivered by a TPA, and the cost is typically offset by savings in payroll taxes and forfeited employee deductions under the "use it or lose it" rule. Any interest earned on positive balances is normally retained by the TPA or the employer, depending on the scope of the services agreement. The employer sets the plan year timeline and maximum amount that may be contributed by each employee.

The primary area of concern for employers is the at-risk provision associated with the FSA. The at-risk provision requires employers to reimburse employees for incurred eligible expenses up to the full amount elected, regardless of how much has already been contributed through payroll deductions. If the employee accesses the full election and leaves employment before funding the balance, the employer has no recourse to recover the unfunded liability.

As noted previously, the FSA is a COBRA-eligible benefit and can be elected by the employee when he or she terminates employment, though it must be funded with after-tax dollars. Knowledgeable employees will use this provision to ensure they don't leave a positive balance in the FSA.

Health Reimbursement Arrangements

Employees

Health reimbursement arrangements are an employer tool and operate according to IRS Section 105 regulations. They're used for the tax-preferred reimbursement of qualified medical expenses for employees as defined by Section 213(d) of the IRS code or a narrower list of services covered as defined by the employer.

During the plan year, employees access these tax-preferred funds with a debit card or file paper claims. Should an employee have a positive balance in his or her HRA at the end of the plan year, that amount can be rolled over to the following year in full, capped, or completely eliminated, at the employer's discretion. The employee should also provide proof of purchase to the HRA administrator to verify the funds were spent on eligible medical expenses.

If an employee terminates employment during the plan year, coverage for qualifying expenses will end at the date of termination. The HRA is a COBRA-eligible benefit and can be elected by the employee when he or she terminates employment.

Employers

HRAs help an employer reimburse employees for qualified medical expenses on a tax-preferred basis. For accounting purposes, HRA funds are essentially treated like health insurance premiums, as business deductions at the point of reimbursement when employers file their tax returns. It's not a salary-reduction plan; however, the employer needs a Section 125 plan document to establish the plan. Once employees incur qualified medical expenses as defined by the employer, the employer reimburses them up to a specified dollar limit. The employer establishes the plan year, determines the maximum amount available by eligibility tier (individual, family, etc.), and also decides whether the HRA funds will roll over, cap at a certain dollar limit, or be eliminated altogether.

Administration of the HRA is usually delivered by a TPA, and the cost is typically determined on a per-participant-per-month fee. Any interest earned on positive balances is normally retained by the TPA or the employer, depending on the scope of the services agreement.

As noted previously, the HRA is a COBRA-eligible benefit and can be elected by the employee when he or she terminates employment. The employer must make a calculation to determine the amount of HRA funds available. Consult your health plan, employee benefits advisor, or tax advisor for assistance.

Health Savings Accounts

Employees

Health savings accounts are an employer and employee tool, and they operate according to IRS Section 223 regulations. They're individually owned bank accounts used for the tax-preferred reimbursement of qualified medical expenses for employees as defined by Section 213(d) of the IRS code.

Employers and employees can contribute to the HSA. During the plan year, employees access these tax-preferred funds with a debit card or check.

Should an employee have a positive balance in his or her HSA at the end of the plan year, that amount is rolled over in full and can be used for future healthcare expenses. The employee should also retain proof of purchase to verify the funds were spent on eligible medical expenses. Unlike the FSA and HRA, receipt verification isn't mandatory, but receipts should be retained for audit purposes.

The employee deposits money (contributed by both the employer and the employee) into a savings account, manages this money, invests it, and collects tax-free interest. This type of account puts employees in charge of making financial decisions. There's a direct correlation between making responsible decisions and saving money, so members should use the education they've received to make informed healthcare choices.

If employees terminate employment during the plan year, they take their HSAs with them to spend as they see fit. The HSA itself isn't a COBRA-eligible benefit.

Employers

HSAs help an employee pay for qualified medical expenses on a tax-preferred basis. Contributions made by the employer to the employee's HSA are a tax-deductible business expense.

The employee contributions to the HSA are normally set up as a salary reduction plan. To qualify for the deduction, the employer needs a Section 125 plan document to establish the plan. Once employees incur qualified medical expenses, they can pay for or reimburse themselves with the funds in the account. The employer chooses an HSA custodian, determines the funding amount for employees by eligibility tier (individual, family, etc.), and also determines the frequency of employer contribution.

Administration of the HSA must be delivered by a qualified HSA custodian, which can either be a banking institution or an insurance company. The bank or insurance company will typically charge an account setup fee and a per-participant-per-month fee.

Any interest earned on positive balances is retained by the account owner, and the funds can be invested as well.

The HSA isn't a COBRA-eligible benefit, but employees take any positive balances with them when they terminate employment.

A Step Ahead

The primary objective of continuous education is to ensure that employees are comfortable using their CDHP. Don't wait for problems to arise: be proactive about keeping employees informed. Schedule group meetings or provide companywide resources if you notice problematic trends or knowledge gaps. Lean on your employee benefits consultant, health plan, and TPA for resources and support to fill in those gaps.

A good way for leadership to keep abreast of the transition process is to hold regularly scheduled meetings with your HR team for the first few months of CDHP implementation. Your HR team will be fielding a lot of questions, so they'll have a good sense of what issues are causing employees difficulty and which areas they have a handle on. Based on these meetings, you can arrange further educational sessions to guide employees through their blind spots.

Employee education meetings will encourage further stages of CDHP adoption. If your employees were initially cautious and decided to start off with an FSA, a healthcare account that doesn't offer the financial rollover benefits of HRAs and HSAs, their increased comfort with their plan will help them move forward to the next step in the CDHP migration process.

Continuous Promotion

To encourage CDHP progression, sponsor focus groups to present information about the implementation stages of CDHPs. Use the communication methods previously discussed, such as educational brochures, online resources, slide presentations, and media clips. In consultation with your employee benefits consultant, insurance provider, and TPA, anticipate specific concerns employees may have about the next stages, and ensure that the presentations and the literature you hand out address these issues. Finally, make knowledgeable personnel available for consultation. Whether they're HR team members, your employee benefits consultant, or contacts at the insurance company, it's important that employees feel that reliable and trustworthy people are available to them, and that no questions will go unanswered.

The Value of Continuing Education

Continuing education is a significant part of successfully adopting a CDHP. The reasons for continuing education after implementation are countless and varied. Newly enrolled members are embarking on a different approach to health care, and even after coaching sessions and education meetings, expect an adjustment period. As members begin to apply the theory learned in a class- room environment to their real health needs and expenses, they'll encounter circumstances that don't always fit into the mold of what they were taught.

Maintaining the effort to educate employees about health and well-being will keep the goals of CDHPs and worksite wellbeing front and center and will continue to motivate them. It's not enough to teach them why they should focus on their health and then leave the matter up to them. Within a few months, resolve will weaken and employees will slowly return to bad habits. Keeping up with education sessions about health and well-being initiatives such as healthy eating and posting new recipes in the kitchen will remind staff to eat well. Providing membership discounts to gyms and organizing office activities will urge them to stay active. Organizing pools to see who can quit smoking or go without junk food the longest will help employees stick with improved lifestyle choices. It's critical that these efforts aren't abandoned after the first few months. Employees should always be reminded in positive ways of why they should be healthier, and how they can achieve their health and well-being goals.

The transition from an attitude of reliance and entitlement to one of independence and responsibility doesn't happen overnight, and you'll have put systems in place to support employees during this potentially trying time. Education seminars, focus groups, and lunch and learns can address widespread challenges, such as difficulty finding information about generic medications. If employees are unable to research drug alternatives and have to pay for brand-name medication, the shock they receive when paying for drugs at the pharmacy will leave them wondering why they chose to pay for medical services out of their healthcare accounts or own pockets. An education session about prescription drugs and online tools like GoodRx.com can educate employees about the money they've saved in lower premiums and the value of their healthcare accounts. You can help them understand that they're now using those premium savings to fund their healthcare expenses. Direct them to reliable sources of information about generic alternatives that can save them thousands of dollars and reaffirm their faith in CDHPs.

Your consistent effort to communicate with your staff throughout the plan year will keep them informed. The more informed and comfortable they are, the easier they'll find it to take the next step in the CDHP journey.

Case Study: *Big Business Investment in Health and Well-Being Pays Off*

Even to the most dedicated management team, implementing an effective, tailored health and well-being strategy that appeals to the majority of a large corporation's employees can sound like a daunting task. Yet the job is doable. If you manage a considerable number of employees, your approach to health and well-being will be the same as that of a smaller company; you'll just have more people to manage. As in any other area of business, the ability to scale by implementing tested processes and using best practices will be important.

Ken's Foods, one of the largest manufacturers of salad dressing and sauces in the United States, employs more than 900 people in three states. The company's senior management team is passionate about promoting a healthy workplace culture, and determined to overcome a unique set of challenges in order to implement worksite health and well-being programs at all of its business locations.

Ken's Foods' employee population is multilingual (most employees are of Asian or Hispanic origin), and employees tend to hold diverse beliefs and opinions about personal health. Not only was communication a challenge for management, there was also no prior history of worksite health and wellness programs at the company. As a result, employees' reactions to new initiatives were unpredictable. To complicate matters further, staff work in one of three daily shifts, so local managers had to ensure that any health and wellness initiatives were equally available to those working on each shift.

continued

The logistical concerns of implementing worksite health and wellness programs that would be meaningful to the diverse populations in each location was a challenge that needed to be carefully mapped out for ultimate success. Management's first step was to conduct environmental and cultural assessments through electronic and paper-based surveys at each of their company locations. From the surveys, management learned that a great number of their employees were regular tobacco smokers. This information was supported by the utilization reports provided by their employee benefits consultant. To immediately address this health concern, Ken's began with a multi-year smoking cessation program. The strategy was built to educate tobacco users of the health risk of tobacco and how to change behavior and maintain a tobacco-free lifestyle. In addition, Ken's created a financial incentive through a tobacco-related premium differential that would reward non-tobacco users. A big part of the multi-year strategy was a graduated complete ban of tobacco use on company grounds.

Ken's chose to share the results of the employee wellness interest survey with all employees. The purpose in doing so was to gather information on employee preferences for future wellness initiatives. The survey was available in two languages at each location, and was offered both digitally and by hard copy. A wellness committee, with representatives in each state, was formed, and HR professionals in each location became wellness team leaders. Senior management then partnered with their employee benefits consultant to get an actuarial consultant and a registered nurse to analyze the company's medical and prescription claims. These consultants provided customized recommendations in collaboration with insurance providers to help improve employee health, and thereby minimize claims resulting from poor lifestyle choices.

Ken's Foods' initial wellness plan was the product of careful design and ongoing consultation. The next steps are detailed in the following.

Biometric screening. Ken's implemented a "Know Your Numbers" campaign, which emphasizes the importance of knowing one's own blood pressure, cholesterol, and blood sugar numbers. A biometric screening and education event allowed employees to learn their personal blood pressure, cholesterol, and blood glucose levels. An incentive program was introduced as part of this campaign in which

continued

employees were offered a $25 gift card as a reward for participating. Employee participation eventually reached 95%. All at-risk individuals (those with elevated readings) were referred to appropriate physicians for follow-up treatment and care.

Self-care. The self-care campaign aimed to educate employees on the various ways in which they could take their health into their own hands. The program was designed to provide employees with in-depth resources so they could be better informed about their health care and lifestyle choices. A few specific examples: information was provided on how to stay fit and healthy by developing a regular sleep routine, eating a healthy diet, going for a walk at lunch, or parking your car in the lot farther away from the building's entrance.

Fitness. A walking program and a fitness education campaign were implemented at each business location. Insurance providers offered individual pedometers to each participant, and intercompany competitions were created to get employees engaged. Ken's Foods offered plenty of encouragement and raffle prizes during the program.

Smoking cessation. The company offered an eight-week on-site smoking cessation workshop in all locations and invited spouses to participate as well. An ongoing smoking cessation education campaign continues to be part of Ken's culture and is shared with all newly hired employees. Ken's remains highly committed and vigilant to keeping their environment tobacco-free.

Stress management. The price of stressed out employees has moved to the forefront of concern for Ken's management team. The cause of stress for most employees comes from on- and off-the-job responsibilities. Ken's started a formal stress-management program with a special summer program that was designed to bring awareness of stress-related health issues through various communication efforts. One effort was focused on providing easy-to-read information and a flyer on stress factors along with some coping strategies.

Nutrition. Since Ken's has physical kitchens and eating areas at all locations, they have incorporated ways to teach their employees about nutrition and healthy eating. They provided employees with important information on the positive impact of eating fruits and vegetables on a daily basis.

continued

The initial response to Ken's health and wellness program was overwhelmingly positive, and in the years since it began, the wellness program has evolved in a number of ways, as part of an ongoing conversation with employees. The wellness plan has moved to a well-being plan and has become more comprehensive and far more personalized. It promotes individual changes in behavior meant to target a specific employee's desired health outcomes, such as personal nutrition and weight reduction. One particularly innovative feature of the plan enables employees to earn higher contributions toward premium payments from the company, based on progress toward specific health goals. Under this system, the employee who smokes tobacco and does not take advantage of a cessation program pays a certain percentage of the premium, which is higher than a nonsmoker. An employee who participates in the biometrics and begins the coaching process to quit smoking and improve the biometric numbers pays a lower percentage. An employee who continues the coaching and engages at regular checkpoints pays a still lower percentage.

The numbers suggest that the enthusiastic employee responses to the program over the years are now backed up by measurable positive results. In a recent year more than 325 employees posted lower body-weight numbers, and 56 who initially reported high LDL levels moved out of the high-risk category.

Ken's Foods' management team has consistently received positive feedback from employees about the evolving and continuously enhanced wellness programs. They are well on their way to achieving a culture shift from one of health and wellness to one of health and well-being. Morale and productivity are up, and employees' overall health has improved. Senior management feels they have overcome major obstacles, and have proved that even large corporations with multiple locations can implement successful health and well-being programs, and positively impact future claims experience.

10

The CDHP Renewal Solution

Great Expectations

As the anniversary of your company's CDHP renewal approaches, you'll want to evaluate the plan's performance. To determine the plan's success, you must weigh expectations against results, taking into account your expectations as a business leader and the expectations of your employees as CDHP members. Ask yourself some important questions, and identify what you're doing well, what hasn't worked well, and what you will do differently going forward.

In most cases, the main objective that an employer and employee share when they decide to implement a CDHP strategy is financial savings. Did you achieve that objective? Have employee and company spending gone down? Did most employees finish the year with value or equity rollovers (that is, positive balances in their healthcare accounts)? Are they spending less money on unnecessary expenses?

Improved health and well-being were probably also high on the list of objectives, particularly for your employees. Are employees making better life-style choices? Do they feel they're healthier and more active than they were when they first enrolled in the CDHP? Do you feel their new attitude has given them more energy and has increased workplace productivity? Has it contributed to a sense of community among your staff?

Increased awareness of healthcare costs is an important objective of the CDHP solution. Has CDHP education enlightened you and your employees about the dangers of blind healthcare spending? Are your employees more self-aware and responsible when it comes to their spending? Does the principle of responsibility effectively reinforce the importance of becoming engaged, educated, and empowered as a healthcare consumer?

If you can answer "yes" to most of these questions, you're on the road to realizing your CDHP's full potential. If the company or your employees have had challenges meeting some of these objectives, remember that this is an evolutionary change rather than a revolutionary one. There's still time to correct your course. This chapter will explain how to analyze your CDHP's performance to ensure you're on the right track to achieve your financial and health and well-being goals.

Gathering and Studying the Data

On a quarterly and annual basis, your employee benefits consultant or your insurer should provide you with information to help you understand how your health plan is performing. You may have access to statistics about the year's usage and medical spending, which will help you identify any medical management opportunities.

In most states, if your organization has fewer than fifty eligible employees (some states below one hundred), your health plan is community rated. As a result, your claims experience doesn't have an impact on renewal. If your organization has fifty-one or more eligible employees, some of your claims experience will factor into your renewal.

In the following section, we discuss how to analyze the data.

Healthcare Trend

Healthcare renewal analysis takes the healthcare trend (medical cost inflation) into consideration. As noted previously, a trend is made up of primarily two components: The first is unit cost, which is the actual cost of each health service or product accessed by employees, such as visits to health services providers, filled prescriptions, or medical equipment. The second is units of service or utilization, which is the number of times a medical service is accessed or a product is purchased; the more times your employees visit the doctor, the more units of service you'll notice when examining plan data.

Claims Experience

Claims experience is the sum of all employee-consumed healthcare products and services. In most markets, employers with over fifty eligible employees will have some of their organization's claims experience factored into their renewal. This is meaningful for groups with over one hundred employees, as the credibility of that claims experience is a bigger factor in their overall renewal. Essentially, CDHPs are designed to discourage overutilization, the overuse of units of service, and create a shift in unit cost purchasing by selecting less expensive options

When employees have good access to information and cost, and are empowered to make informed decisions, their use of health services and products will be reduced to what is necessary, not what is convenient. Simply comparing costs—those incurred this year under your CDHP to those incurred last year under a traditional health plan—will reveal only part of the picture. If your costs have decreased significantly, you might be tempted to close the books and pat yourself on the back for a job well done. But wouldn't you want to know how you and your employees could save even more money and become even healthier? Identifying trends in your claims experience can be illuminating, and will help you proactively address the issues that ariseEven if your business has experienced some financial savings by changing to a CDHP, closely inspecting detailed health plan data may reveal that additional coaching could save even more. Perhaps units of service have decreased significantly. Employees have learned that they don't need a doctor's opinion for every runny nose. If unit costs remain pretty close to last year's, there may be a problem with your education strategy. Perhaps employees who rely on necessary prescription medication are uninformed about the efficacy of generic drugs, so they're paying three or more times as much for the name-brand variety. Or maybe employees aren't focusing on preventive care, so the cost of their eventual medical treatment is greater.

Analyzing your claims experience can uncover problematic areas and allow you to address them before the next plan year. In this case, you might schedule an additional educational meeting devoted exclusively to the effectiveness and safety of generic drugs. Employees' doubts will be eased significantly if they learn that generic drugs must undergo the same testing as name-brand ones before they're approved for sale. Targeted educational meetings can address problems identified in your company's claims experience.

Being aware of what's driving your claims experience will allow you to bridge gaps in employee awareness wherever necessary. One education session could lead to big unit cost decreases, and therefore increased savings in the form of improved claims experience, for your employees and for you. By ensuring that both unit costs and units of service have decreased since implementing your CDHP, you're ensuring the success of one of the plan's most exciting features—the ability to lower healthcare costs by becoming a more informed consumer.

Premium Increases

With any health insurance plan, you can expect rate increases. To evaluate the rate increases you've been subject to as a traditional health insurance customer, gather your renewal analyses from the past several years. You'll probably find that, on average, your premium cost has increased 8% to 12% per year (varying considerably by region across the United States). This means that in five years, your premium costs may have almost doubled. On the other hand, CDHP premium increases are usually lower. Over time, that difference compounds and can add up to considerable savings.

So how do CDHPs keep your premium increases lower? Contrary to what most people believe, premium rate increases aren't determined entirely by uncontrollable forces such as inflation and general cost increases. While these forces do make up some of the increase, part of the overall increase is completely independent of these factors, and can be reduced through behavior change. With CDHPs, you can adjust more financial levers to moderate your final rate of increase. These levers include your deductible, coinsurance, and healthcare account funding allocation.

Deductible Leveraging

In a traditional health insurance plan, 100% of your contribution goes toward the plan's premium. In a CDHP, roughly 80% of the plan's cost funds the insurance premium, while part of the other 20% (usually half) is invested in a healthcare account for each of your employees and their families. The remaining percentage is a direct result of deductible leveraging, and represents the financial impact a higher deductible has on total premiums. Deductible leveraging is the practice of increasing the deductible each year to counterbalance overall healthcare inflation.

Deductible leveraging can be more beneficial if you adjust your employees' deductible from time to time to help you pay less to your health insurer. The healthcare account's inherent ability to grow in value/equity allows you to adjust the CDHP's deductible and keep the relative value of your health plan consistent from year to year for most employees. The CDHP allows you to invest the premium savings in the healthcare accounts for your employees and watch their value/equity grow over time.

Coinsurance

Coinsurance is the percentage of medical costs employees are responsible for paying above their deductible. Normally, this financial lever is associated with a PPO, a health plan that gives members the choice of in- and out-of-network providers and doesn't require designating a primary care doctor. For example, your coinsurance level in-network might be 100%, which means plan members aren't responsible for expenses beyond their deductible. When they seek care from an out-of-network provider, members may have a coinsurance level of 80%, which means they'll be responsible for 20% of medical costs up to a coinsurance limit, such as $5,000, or a maximum of $1,000 in out-of-pocket costs. This type of plan design would be called 100/80 coinsurance with a $5,000 coinsurance limit.

In the early stages of your CDHP design and adoption, you might want to use the 100/80 design so that your members have less to learn. As you and your employees become more comfortable with the plan, you can move this lever down and reduce premium costs by introducing additional out-of-pocket responsibility in the form of coinsurance, such as 90/70 or 10% member responsibility above the deductible.

Healthcare Account Funding

The amount of funding you put into your healthcare account is also a significant lever in the financial structure of your CDHP. To properly design a CDHP, part of the premium savings (usually 50% if properly structured) generated from the HDHP must be invested in funding healthcare accounts for the company's employees to spend on qualified medical expenses below the deductible. The amount funded can and should vary by family size (i.e., single, two-party, and family) and is variable from year to year.

The healthcare account is the CDHP's most flexible feature because the annual amount of funding can be adjusted based on employee utilization, and adjusted down to a specific dollar level (rather than being locked into a health plan's limited design flexibility). The funding amounts can't be individualized or the plan will risk discrimination, which is prohibited by federal regulation. Instead, when your employee benefits consultant and your health insurer provide overall utilization data and information by data enrollment category (i.e., individual, two-party, family), your funding allocation decisions will become more apparent. The healthcare account data will help you determine the appropriate adjustments to make from year to year.

The Year in Review

Once you've analyzed the important factors affecting health plan performance, it's time to examine the factors in your workplace and the marketplace that may also affect your CDHP's long-term viability. Consider any changes your business has gone through over the past year and any shifts in the marketplace or global and national economies that have affected spending or will affect spending in the coming year. Ask yourself the following questions to determine what changes should be made to effectively manage your renewal.

- **Has our business experienced any financial or structural changes?**

   Based on your business's performance and financial situation over the previous year, you may need to cut back on expenses, or you may be able to offer your employees more benefits through additional healthcare account funding. Consider your budget constraints and requirements before beginning the renewal process so you can ask your employee benefits consultant and your insurer the right questions.

- **Has our company hired or reduced a significant number of employees?**

   If you've hired new staff or had a reduction by renewal time, chances are they've changed the average age of your group and haven't yet been educated about CDHPs. If you have hired new staff, you may want to organize a second round of introductory education meetings before open enrollment takes place. Discuss with your employee benefits consultant and your health insurer any concerns you have about increased or decreased CDHP membership.

- **Are there any prominent medical trends among our employees?**

  Are you noticing a general improvement in your employees' health and the performance of your claims experience? If so, that's great news. Be sure to praise members who are doing well, and encourage everyone to keep making the effort. If you notice troubling health trends (e.g., many of your employees are being treated for high blood pressure), implement targeted education programs in the workplace and help get the problem under control.

- **What are employees saying?**

  If your employees' response to the CDHP solution has been mostly positive, consider that a marker of success. If there have been some negative reactions, take the time to get insight and see where more education is needed. If you haven't heard anything at all, you've got a problem. To make your plan a success, you must know how your employees feel—CDHPs are designed to engage the consumer. Encourage employees to share their CDHP experiences so that you're aware of any significant concerns before you finalize your renewal and plan offering for open enrollment. Speak to your employee benefits consultant or your health insurer if you need additional guidance.

- **How is HR handling the transition?**

  If your HR team is dealing with significant or recurring problems, you may need to change your education efforts or administrative procedures. Find out how HR is managing well before renewal and open enrollment takes place. This will allow you to make any needed educational and procedural changes before you consult with your health insurance provider.

- **Have there been any federal or state regulatory changes that might affect the type of coverage your company offers?**

    Regulatory changes can help your company by augmenting the product offerings and flexibility available to you. Your options may be improved, such as implementing a health plan premium contribution strategy that rewards non-smokers or those who participate in an approved wellness program. Regulatory changes can also create new laws that may hurt your budget, plan design, and administrative operations. For instance, at the time this book is being written, the federal government is debating the repeal and replacement of the Affordable Care Act and other regulatory changes that may positively impact the value of healthcare accounts in the health insurance system. With that said, it's important to be aware of any new regulations before making big decisions about the year ahead. Your employee benefits consultant can help.

- **Has the marketplace changed?**

    Perhaps your health insurer has begun offering new CDHP products that may be a better fit for you and your employees. Perhaps more competitors have entered the market over the year, and your health insurance provider will be offering attractive pricing and more enhancements to improve overall value. These outside factors are worth researching because they can give you the upper hand in negotiations during your renewal.

You can pose many other important questions in preparation for renewal, so ask your employee benefits consultant about them. It's impossible to enter the renewal process with too much information, so gather as much insight as possible before making a decision about your insurer or the CDHP you'll offer to your employees.

Making Choices
Healthcare Account Funding

At renewal, you can decide whether you want to fund more, less, or the same amount of contribution toward health insurance premiums or the healthcare account to help employees and their families pay for the deductible. In the case of HRAs, you can also decide whether to enhance your plan by offering additional coverage for services, such as dental or eye care, that can be funded with healthcare account dollars deposited in a limited-purpose FSA. Though you made similar decisions when you first designed and enrolled your employees in a CDHP, your decisions will now be based on actual usage.

Depending on your region, your health insurance carrier, and the size of your group (usually over one hundred eligible employees), your insurer can supply you with information about how much your employees have spent on healthcare costs that year and what kinds of health services they accessed. At a minimum, you should review healthcare account usage information to identify any patterns that must be addressed through additional education or a health and wellness program. This will help you determine if the healthcare account funding allocation you offer employees is appropriate or needs to be adjusted. Based on this information, you can determine whether you've been contributing too much, too little, or just enough to the plan.

When you implement a CDHP/HRA using a QHDHP as the high-deductible health plan that covers preventive care at 100% and funds 50% of the plan's deductible through the HRA, on average you'll see 60% of the total healthcare account funding allocation exhausted from year to year. On the other hand, if you use an HDHP that subjects only high-cost medical care to the deductible and not the routine day-to-day medical care of doctors and prescription drugs, that usage figure will decrease to about 40%.

When you implement a CDHP/HSA using a QHDHP as the high-deductible health plan that covers preventive care at 100% and you fund 25% to 50% of the deductible, on average you'll see usage decrease even further to roughly 40% of the HSA funding allocation. In most cases, the drop in usage with the CDHP/HSA is substantially greater than the CDHP/HRA and underscores the principle of "use it or keep it."

Too Much Funding

If most employees have a significant amount of healthcare account funding from the previous year to roll over into the next, they may be receiving more funding than they need. In the first plan year, this isn't necessarily a bad thing because there's more risk in the first year, and allocating more funds may actually help a majority of employees feel the positive effects of the "use it or keep it" principle that's so integral to behavioral change. Still, it's important to examine spending patterns to determine the reason for the above-average rollover.

You may be contributing too much, but it's also possible that members have had an unusually lucky year and may experience the opposite in the coming plan year. Remember that you don't want to penalize employees for cutting down on their healthcare spending by reducing funding. Your employee benefits consultant and your insurer can help you assess the relevant factors to determine if the phenomenon is an anomaly, if it appears to be the result of preven- tive care and alternative treatment, or if you've overestimated your contribution levels. They'll help you adjust accordingly.

Too Little Funding

It's possible that your employees have had to spend a lot of money out-of-pocket because your company's contribution was inadequate, maybe because you didn't invest enough of the premium savings from the transition to an HDHP. Perhaps you overestimated the effects of a health and wellness program in the early stages and assumed that spending would go down more than it has, or perhaps you didn't yet have a realistic handle on the cost of health care. Your employee benefits consultant and your insurer can help you identify the underlying trends and give you insight to help you make the best decisions as you move forward.

If your organization experiences greater usage of the healthcare account than the averages listed previously, you may need to supply additional dollars to ensure that you haven't shifted too much financial burden to your employees. This second-year adjustment will encourage employees to keep up the good work and let them know that you're in this together and that you'll make corrections when necessary.

In some cases, money isn't the issue, and a funding increase won't solve the problem. Instead, determine if employees have received enough education about reducing spending and improving health, or if they've received this education but aren't motivated enough to apply it. If lack of education is the problem, arrange education meetings with your employee benefits consultant and your insurer to focus on problem areas. If motivation is the issue, let this disappointment serve as an incentive to encourage workplace activities and increased worker health. Organize group activities so that the strongest, most motivated employees can lead by example. Don't leave it entirely up to your staff to change their lifestyles—improve the health of their work environment and show them by example the benefits of the CDHP philosophy.

An Appropriate Amount

You might find that the amount you've been contributing to the plan has been right on the mark and consistent with the statistics provided previously. On average, roughly 65% of employees should roll over funds from year to year, roughly 25% will exhaust their healthcare account funding but not satisfy their deductible, and approximately 10% will exhaust their account funding, satisfy the deductible, and hit their maximum out-of-pocket. Most employees will have some rollover (a good thing), and some will have had to pay for some of their medical expenses out-of-pocket (which is unavoidable). If these two extremes are reasonably balanced, you'll know you've found an appropriate contribution level and should work to maintain it. Over the years, however, employee needs will change and you may have to contribute more or less to the healthcare account. The purpose of an annual review of your CDHP is to assess your plan's performance and determine any necessary adjustments. Let your employee benefits consultant and insurer help you navigate these important decisions.

The Next Steps

The renewal process should help you decide if your company and staff are ready to advance to the next stage of CDHP involvement. Ultimately, until employees have enrolled in a CDHP/HSA, they aren't making the most of all that CDHPs have to offer.

Based on the data your employee benefits consultant and insurer have provided, you can decide if your company is ready to advance to the next stage of CDHP migration. The advantages of HSAs are compelling, and if the data show that employees are embracing their plan and using healthcare responsibly, it's time for them to reap the rewards. When employees are ready to manage the money in their HSAs wisely, you should be willing to contribute financially to their all-round fiscal and physical well-being.

With an FSA, members enjoy greater purchasing power for your health-care dollar (tax-preferred funding) and responsibility to effectively manage a healthcare account, but they aren't able to save their money. With CDHP/HRAs, member credit can roll over and provide them with additional medical coverage, but they still aren't accumulating savings. With CDHP/HSAs, members enjoy all the advantages of FSAs and HRAs, as well as the ability to maintain a vehicle for building equity that belongs to them personally to pay for future healthcare expenses.

Education Year after Year

Facilitating the transition to an HSA will require ongoing education. Hopefully, the educational resources and personnel will still be at hand from the previous year's shift to CDHPs. With this framework in place, half the work is done—employees are familiar with the system, are willing to attend educational meetings, and know who to go to for additional help and information. Now you simply have to introduce new material highlighting the differences between a CDHP/HRA and a CDHP/HSA, and to teach members how to maximize the benefits that HSAs provide.

Spreading the News

After you've had a renewal consultation with your employee benefits consultant or your insurer, he or she will present some plan design options. If any changes are made to the benefit structure, the new plan design details should be presented to all employees. Call their attention to information about renewal rates, administrative changes, any modifications to administrative procedures (e.g., claim reimbursement), and anything else pertinent to their use of the plan. Generally, employees will be given two to four weeks during open enrollment to review their plan design choices before any changes take effect. There are administrative procedures to factor in, as well as the issuance of insurance identification cards, so allow enough time for all parties to review the terms and conditions of their plan options.

Knowing your stats, or obtaining information from your employee benefits consultant or insurer, is an invaluable resource during your renewal period. Armed with actual statistics about your company's CDHP, you'll be prepared to discuss all renewal options with your employee benefits consultant or your insurer, and you'll help your employees choose from the best possible solutions by allowing them to suggest options based on your plan's unique performance. Take the time to prepare a renewal strategy with your employee benefits consultant before you meet with your insurer, and be open to any recommendations. Times change, your needs change, and the inherent flexibility of the CDHP is designed to keep up.

Case Study: *Plan Design*

Havens is an independent private school employing 120 faculty and staff. Between 209 and 2014, its health insurance premiums rose steadily by 12% to 15% each year. After payroll, employee benefits are generally the second largest expense for any organization, and healthcare represents about 80% of those total costs. In today's market, independent schools face many financial challenges, including endowment shrinkage, declining donor support, student attrition, a tightening credit market, and budget constraints. With these limitations on spending, Havens had to do something, and the school didn't want to let go of faculty or staff.

In 2015, the school made a progressive decision to attack its healthcare cost increases by offering CDHP on a full-replacement basis, eliminating its HMO options completely.

Though many of its peers were making this transition over three years, Havens decided it would be easier to transition all faculty and staff together in one year. Making such a drastic change created its own challenges, but Havens was on a mission to engage and educate faculty and staff on the new CDHP and to encourage them to embrace change. This attitude helped the school address almost everyone's misgivings, and those who weren't entirely convinced came around once they became familiar with the plan and witnessed the rewards.

Havens's plan was structured as a PPO/HDHP insurance plan. The PPO arrangement gives members the freedom to choose their providers because they have in-network and out-of-network coverage and don't need referrals. The plan featured a $1,500 qualified high deductible for individuals and a $3,000 deductible for families, with 100% coinsurance in-network and 80% coinsurance out-of-network. The school funded 50% of the deductible through the HRA and allowed unused funds to roll over from year to year, capping the total accumulation at the annual deductible.

continued

The first year Havens implemented this plan, it saved $69,900, equivalent to the salary of a full-time faculty member. In the second year, Havens's rate increase was only 6%, compared to 15% on the traditional health plan. The third year garnered the most significant savings, with a rate increase of only 1%, compared to the whopping 25% increase Havens could have expected from its traditional insurance provider.

By adopting a CDHP, Havens has been able to curtail one of its largest expenses, allowing school leaders to use the significant financial savings for the school's operating budget.

11

The Report Card

The Payoff

Everyone at your business has worked hard to implement a high-performing health insurance plan, one that offers employees and their families a comprehensive benefits package as well as a return on their healthcare investment. The road from a traditional insurance plan to CDHP adoption will have its ups and downs, but soon you'll see how well your hard work has paid off. Your employees will enjoy their new opportunities as they take better care of their physical and financial well-being. In short, your CDHP will work, and your preparation for this new healthcare strategy will be the reason why.

The CDHP solution isn't designed to benefit only employees—business owners should benefit from premium cost savings, cost aversion, and a healthier workforce. Part of the renewal process involves analyzing your company's financial savings, and the report card assesses how well your company performed over the course of the year. With help from your employee benefits consultant and insurer, you'll discover where you've excelled, as well as areas that could use some further improvement.

Getting Prepared

To make the analysis as easy and straightforward as possible, you will want to get your financial leadership team involved. It is important to examine your organization's fiscal performance from the previous year and determine which parts of it were affected by your new health plan. With their help, you can compare the CDHP's results to the goals and objectives you set early in the year, and determine whether those goals have been met. The team will be familiar with your organization's financials, allowing them to advise you on how to support your current health plan strategy. They'll suggest adjustments to the overarching business strategy to make your health plan costs as low as possible, while continuing to offer comprehensive benefits to employees. Also, your financial team will know which questions to ask and what goals to set to make your coming year even better than the last.

It's a good idea to meet with your financial and HR teams before sitting down with your employee benefits consultant and insurer so you enter that discussion with an agenda. Any decisions made at the meeting are guaranteed to affect the HR and finance departments, so having all stakeholders present will eliminate the need to go back and forth to iron out the kinks.

Tackling the Issues

The more successful the plan is for your employees, the more successful it is for you, the employer. As employees learn how to maximize their plan's benefits and as enthusiasm for plan adoption spreads, your financial reward will continue to grow. Employees will take fewer sick days, and their productivity will increase. Overall, your employees' comfort, understanding, and enthusiasm for CDHPs are the foundation of a successful implementation.

It might be a good idea to survey employees after the plan is installed to find out how they feel about the plan in general: Are their overall feelings negative or positive? Have they been recommending adoption to their colleagues? The responses you get to general questions will give you a sense of how employees are enjoying the plan and allow you to ask pertinent, specific questions.

If responses are overwhelmingly positive, ask members what communication and education approaches they found particularly effective and use those to appeal to new hires and employees who haven't yet enrolled. If members are having problems adjusting to the new health plan, identify problem areas and address these specifically. A small problem at the core of the educational experience can define how employees feel about their plans, and if you don't identify and tackle these issues, an easily solved problem can have far-reaching effects. By taking initiative and detecting these issues early, you increase the chances of successful continued use of CDHPs.

After discussing your employees' reactions to their first year of CDHP use, follow up with focus sessions of a cross-section of employees and then a meeting with your employee benefits consultant and insurer. They should be able to offer tried-and-true solutions to any problems you may have; although it's your first time dealing with these issues, they've helped dozens of clients through these same processes. They know the most effective way to deal with problems, and you should take advantage of this valuable resource.

Forward Thinking—Sustainability versus Growth

Once you've established where you currently stand, decide what you'd like to accomplish with your CDHP over the next few years. Set short- and long-term goals, and then assess your current plan with your employee benefits consultant and insurer to determine if it can help you deliver your goals and expectations. Health care will continue to evolve, and you can expect that in five years it will be in a different state. Will your plan evolve into one that will deliver over the long term? Part of this development occurs naturally, as more people enroll in the CDHP and employees become progressively healthier and more responsible for their health and healthcare spending. However, you can put strategies in place to encourage plan development.

Employees must be taught how to be healthcare consumers. They'll most likely doubt that they can take control of their healthcare spending and make it more efficient. They'll likely focus on catastrophic scenarios, such as heart attacks, and terminal diseases, such as cancer, to underscore their concern about their ability to control their health and healthcare spending. The CDHP solution covers such events and limits financial exposure to the employee. We call these moments "teaching moments," and when they occur, it's up to you, your staff, employee benefits consultant, and insurer to show employees how much they can do.

Provide examples that employees frequently encounter and where they can be in full control. Most employees probably had a routine cold over the past year or so; should they have gone to the doctor, or is there a home remedy they could have used? When their children are sick, should they use an urgent care facility, use the telemedicine option, or go to their primary care physicians or a specialist? When they need prescription drugs, are there generic drugs they can purchase instead of the brand-name equivalents? When riding bicycles, do they wear helmets or just hope they won't fall and get seriously injured? In each example, making the right choice can increase an employee's ability to roll over dollars into employee healthcare accounts. Show employees that they can save substantially when they and their family members make more informed purchasing decisions over a long period. There's value in the compounding effect of the money in their healthcare accounts.

It's vital that your staff be apprised of all developments. Your goals and theirs should complement each other, so always consider which actions will help the company reach its goals, and share this information with them. Without your staff's full cooperation and enthusiasm, they won't achieve their goals and you can't reach yours, so ensure that members are prepared for any future changes and are comfortable with them before they're implemented. To guarantee this, put someone in charge of maintaining education and health and well-being initiatives so that these continue to be engaging, dynamic, and effective.

Setting goals, formulating strategies, and informing employees will enhance the performance of your CDHP. A little work can go a long way in this respect. A major part of the CDHP philosophy involves taking control and being responsible, so practice what you preach. You can't expect your employees to embrace values that you yourself disregard, so be proactive and set a positive example. By taking control of your health plan's performance and making it work for you, you pave the road ahead for your employees and encourage them to take steps to improve their physical and financial well-being, as well as your own.

Case Study: *Big Savings for Small Business*

Debbie and Mike lead an employee benefits firm that employs forty-six people. Realizing their HMO insurance product was quickly making their health insurance costs unsustainable, Mike and Debbie decided to reevaluate their company's strategy. After six years of offering employees an HMO, and coping with consistent premium cost increases of up to 12% per year, they transitioned to a CDHP paired with a health savings account. Because the insurer classified Debbie and Mike's company as a small group (less than 50 employees), the group's actual use of the plan didn't have any impact on their premium increases. Instead, their health insurance provider used an underwriting methodology called community rating. In other words, premium requirements are based on the employer's demographics and the insurer's total book of business, and not on the needs of their small company.

continued

With some careful planning, Debbie and Mike came to understand that small businesses face unique challenges in the health insurance marketplace: their impact on product pricing is limited, and factors beyond their control will almost always determine their premium increases.

Debbie and Mike didn't want to pass double-digit health insurance cost increases on to their employees and their families—that kind of thinking went against their company philosophy. After investigating their options, they realized that cost reduction could come only from a health insurance product that they could tailor to fit their needs. They also wanted everyone at their company to work together to manage costs and improve their overall health.

In 2006, Mike and Debbie eliminated their company's HMO option and became pioneers in the use of CDHP/HSA. The plan evolved over time (as well-managed CDHPs do) and now incorporates a $3,100 deductible for individuals and a $6,200 deductible for families, and an incentive for employees: the company funds 50% of the deductible through the HSA. Today, the plan features a comprehensive health and well-being program that rewards wellness dollars for making healthy choices—not just in terms of diet and exercise, but also in areas of personal finance, community service, and mindfulness. In addition, the company sponsors a wide range of social events that improves team spirit and collaboration, which in turn gives the employees a sense of belonging and greater engagement in their work.

Debbie and Mike took the time to properly educate their employees about the CDHP and enhanced the program over time based on feedback from the plan participants. Their generosity and commitment was rewarded with employee goodwill. Employees showed their appreciation for the new plan by becoming active participants in their own healthcare decisions, thus maximizing the plan's effectiveness. As a result, Mike and Debbie's company experienced a modest average rate increase of 6% over the last ten years. What's more, their costs were no longer destined to rise with the tides of the nation's healthcare trend. Debbie and Mike had finally found the solution that allowed their small company to positively influence its own health insurance costs and support sustainable, long-term improvements in health and well-being for their employees and families . . . without having to pass dramatic cost increases on to their employees.

12

Health Insurance Financing Strategies

Financing Options

When choosing the best financing strategy for your CDHP, you will want to take a number of factors into account, starting with risk tolerance and risk suitability.

Risk tolerance considers business factors such as the financial strength of your organization, as measured by your financial statements (e.g., profit and loss statement, balance sheet, cash flow projections, etc.). If your finances are challenged, your level of risk tolerance will most likely be diminished. Conversely, if your financials are strong, your level of risk tolerance will probably be higher.

Risk suitability, on the other hand, considers the collective health of your organization by looking at things like demographics: average age of your employee population, male/female mix, industry, geography, and plan history. The most helpful information in determining risk suitability is your organization's claims experience, including large claimants and the ongoing prognosis of those claimants. This information is typically available for underwriting purposes when you have 100 or more employees. (Unfortunately, in most markets, health insurance carriers do not provide relevant information on claims experience when you insure less than 100 employees, which is one of the challenges facing smaller firms.) When underwriters look closely at risk suitability factors, they can assess whether your risk profile best lends itself to taking on risk or transferring it to an insurance company.

There are three core financing vehicles available to organizations when they offer health insurance to their employees and families: fully self-funded financing, fully insured financing, and partially self-funded financing. Let's look at all three of these options.

Option One: Self-Funded Financing

Self-funded plans are most commonly used by employers who employ five hundred or more employee lives. It is typically considered a long-term strategy to achieve savings and greater cost control. Employers of this size are what insurance carriers deem fully credible. The claims experience that these employees and their family members generate are highly predictable because of the size of the covered population. It's the reason insurance is often called the law of large numbers. The bigger the sample size, the more predictable the outcome.

Underwriters or actuaries cannot predict, with total accuracy, the exact nature of the medical situations that will arise or the specific employees who will be affected. What they can do is make informed statistical predictions, based on past history, of the number of incidences of certain types of health conditions that will develop in the group. Underwriters have access to a large enough pool of data to help forecast future exposure.

Employers of this size have a high degree of risk tolerance, and in most cases are suitable to take on the risk because they have a credible pool of experience. Consequently, it's relatively easy for them to assume all the risk of their employees' claims. It follows, then, that if your organization falls into this category and you are opting for a fully self-funded health insurance financing vehicle for your CDHP, you will not need to buy any reinsurance or stop-loss protection. (We'll discuss these terms in a moment.) Your risk pool will be large enough to allow you to accurately predict the claims incurred by your employees and their families and enable you to accurately forecast this risk exposure.

The advantages to self-funding:

1. **Lower administrative and operating costs.** Self-funded plans are typically administered either by an insurance carrier or by a third-party administrator who pays the claims. As a result, the administrative and operating costs are lower than with fully insured financing.

2. **Data control.** Employers with self-funded plans are paying the claims on behalf of their employees and family members. As a result, they retain ownership of all the data and have greater control over plan design, benefits covered, premium contribution, and claims information.

3. **Plan design flexibility and utilization control.** The focus here is on the ability of employers to design a plan that specifically fits the culture and need of the organization. It allows the employer an opportunity to analyze claim utilization and be creative with benefit features that are targeted to improve the overall health and well-being of the group.

4. **Cash flow.** The cost of self-funded plans can be about a third lower than fully insured plans. This is due to the transparent environment that comes from retaining ownership of the risk and data so you can see where every dollar is being spent. Employers pay expenses as they are incurred. What's more, there is little to no profit or margin built into the healthcare inflation factor known as trend. Trend is applied to future claims by the insurance company to calculate the future value of health care in today's dollars. As a result, employers are likely to purchase more efficiently and retain that margin in their own bank account (reserves).

5. **Premium tax.** In most states, premium tax is not applicable under a self-funded plan, which can result in immediate savings to the employer for considering this financing model.

The disadvantages to self-funding include:

1. **Risk management.** Your organization assumes total responsibility for all risk whether or not it has favorable or unfavorable claims experience.

2. **Fiduciary responsibility.** Your organization assumes legal and fiduciary responsibility for claims payment decisions.

3. **Administration.** Your organization assumes all administrative responsibilities for running the plan.

4. **Budget.** These plans can be more difficult to budget, due to the cyclical nature of claims experience and their impact on cash flow.

Option Two: Fully Insured Financing

Fully insured financing has traditionally been the financing mechanism of choice among employers of fewer than 500 employee lives. This is because the smaller the company, the less predictable and more volatile the claim experience becomes and thus the more expensive fully self-insured financing is for the group.

If you opt for such financing, you will provide the carrier with basic information on all the employees and their dependents who will be covered on the plan. This is known as your census. Based on the demographics of that census and on your choice of CDHP plan designs, the carrier will then provide you with an underwritten monthly premium rate. You are then locked into that premium rate for a 12-month period. In exchange, the company transfers all the risk of any claims by its employees and their family members to the insurer. Your claim liability is completely transferred to the insurance company. The organization receives a renewal rate at the end of that contract year and decides whether or not to continue with the same insurer or plan design and premium contribution strategy. It is a year-to-year decision-making process.

The advantages of fully insured financing:

1. **The insurer carries the load.** The plan transfers all risk, fiduciary and legal responsibility, and administration over to the insurer.

2. **Benefits.** The insurer provides you with all state-mandated benefits.

3. **Claims don't affect your premium.** Over the course of the contract, there is a level premium regardless of your claims experience.

4. **Flexibility.** Transitioning between health plans is easier, as reserves are included in the premium and liability is left behind upon termination of the contract (no claims runout exposure).

5. **Budget.** From a cash flow perspective, it's easy to budget for these plans on a monthly and annual basis.

The disadvantages of fully insured financing:

1. **Lack of transparency.** Due to the nature of the contract and the transfer of risk to the insurer, the plan's data becomes the insurance company's property. You, as the employer, will receive limited data for 100–500 employees and no data for less than 100 employees.

2. **Higher cost.** Fully insured financing trends are currently ranging between 8% and 12% across the country, depending on your specific geography, size, and plan type. These trend figures are based on the carrier's contracts with all its healthcare providers, including doctors, hospitals, the government, and prescription drug companies. It's important to note that carrier trends include profit margin. For the companies availing themselves of this financing vehicle, it is difficult to know how much of these margins are real (based on risk charge and inflation), and how much is profit.

3. **Lack of control over pricing.** The carriers use their book of business to create prices for companies to buy insurance for their employees and family members. When your company has less than 250 employees and less than two years of claims experience, the carriers will blend your experience with their book of business to determine your organization's rate. This is called community rating or community rating by class. Because the insurer's rates are based on demographics, minimal claims experience, blended with the carrier's book of business, the employer has no control over the price of the insurance component of the CDHP design.

Option Three: Partially Self-Funded Financing

As discussed previously, companies employing fewer than 500 employee lives have traditionally opted for fully insured financing. These companies typically present a higher degree of volatility than larger companies. This is particularly true of a subsection of the middle market made up of employers of between 50 and 250 employee lives. The claims experience of companies this size is not considered credible. This means it is more challenging for insurers to accurately forecast future claims experience, and forecasts are used to assess risk.

Due to the volatility associated with covering employers of between 50 and 250 lives, the carriers assess substantial charges for the risk that is presented due to the volatile nature of claims experience for groups of that size. As a result, carriers have a higher level of profitability on employers in this segment. In fact, employers are often significantly overcharged for the risk they present.

What can middle-market employers do about that? One option is to adopt a financing strategy called a partially self-funded plan.

A partially self-funded plan gives the employer the protection of being fully insured while also assuming some risk on a self-funded basis. Under this financing vehicle, there is a risk-transfer mechanism built into the contract to protect the employer from any one single claim, and capping their maximum exposure at a predetermined ceiling. Employers have full view of their data and full control over their plan. This is achieved through one of two means: either through traditional stop-loss insurance or through a captive insurance arrangement. Let's further explore each of these risk-management options.

Traditional Stop-Loss Insurance

Employers in the 50–500 market can protect themselves from volatility by purchasing a special kind of insurance called stop-loss or reinsurance. Known technically as specific reinsurance and aggregate reinsurance, or more formally as specific stop-loss and aggregate stop-loss, these reinsurance contracts give protection in the event of one large claim made by one covered member or in the event of a series of claims from all an organization's employees and family members.

For example, if someone in your company is diagnosed with a serious illness and generates $250,000 of claims, at that point specific stop-loss insurance will reimburse the employer for any liability above their specific deductible (let's say $50,000 as an example).

Your organization would pay a set premium to the reinsurer—the stop-loss company—to protect the organization if a catastrophic claim should occur. If such a claim arises, you would pay the claim and subsequently be reimbursed through the stop-loss policy. It's important to note that this is a reimbursement mechanism, not a health insurance plan.

On its own, such a policy would still put an employer at risk for exposure if a large number of employees incurred significant claims. This is where the next level of risk protection takes place, and where the aggregate reinsurance steps in. Aggregate reinsurance is like an umbrella over the entire organization. It stops your liability at a certain point, known as the attachment point. This varies by state; typically it is 120% or 125% of expected claims.

For example, let's assume that in your state the aggregate attachment point is 125%. In this case, the stop-loss carrier might give you an expected claim number of $1 million, meaning that it expects you and the members of your plan to generate $1 million in claims over a twelve-month period. Aggregate reinsurance would cap your liability to 125% of that expected claim number to give you a finite or maximum liability. If you go over $1.25 million in claims in that contract year, the reinsurer will step in and reimburse you above that figure.

Captive Financing Model

Captive insurance, an underutilized option in our view, adds an elegant twist to the traditional stop-loss insurance financing construct through the notion of shared risk and responsibility.

As mentioned previously, companies of a certain size are not considered credible from an actuarial standpoint. Their insurer will agree to take on the risk, but only at an increased risk charge. This means that it can be extremely expensive for an individual company without a credible pool of experience to self-insure. Employers in such a market segment typically do not partially self-insure on their own because the stop-loss premiums they have to pay can be very expensive. This is where the captive financing solution comes into play.

It allows an employer (plan sponsor) to take on a predetermined level (the first $50,000) of risk for each employee and each family member covered on the plan. Claims below $50,000 are the most predictable kinds of claims. This is called self-funded retention; the employer assumes all the risk for the most predictable claims. These claims do not usually relate to life-threatening ailments, and they are comparatively inexpensive, with a wide variation in price, which usually goes undetected until after the service is provided, which contributes to the inefficiency of your healthcare dollars. They include lumps and bumps, aches and pains, minor scrapes, minor breaks and fractures, MRI and CAT scans, X-rays, and prescription drugs.

Captive insurance allows like-minded middle-market organizations (50–500) to share risk for somewhat predictable and somewhat unpredictable claims. These claims could be life-threatening or not, and involve more expensive medical care for services like hip and knee replacements, heart or cancer surgery, expensive medications, and longer hospital stays. This is called the captive layer, and it is shared risk. Once the employer incurs claims that go above the specific stop-loss deductible ($50,000) and below the next threshold of risk ($250,000), the captive layer premiums are drawn down to reimburse that employer.

Each organization posts collateral (reserve) when they join a captive—typically 4%–5% of the annual fully insured premium—just as they do when they use fully insured financing. The difference is the transparency of the process. Why are reserves important? Regulators require them to fund future claims. If or when all funds in the captive layer are exhausted, the collateral is subject to drawdown as well. At that point, the reinsurance carrier assumes the liability for these claims for the remainder of the contract year.

Finally, captive insurance allows middle-market employers to transfer risk for their most unpredictable claims above the program maximum liability—also known as the captive layer attachment point ($300,000). These claims are for comparatively rare services like delivering premature twins, organ transplants, and expensive medications to treat hemophiliacs. This is called the transfer layer. If any claims exceed the self-funded retention and the captive layer, the remainder of that claim risk is assumed by the reinsurer, thereby providing the employer and their like-minded colleagues in the program with catastrophic protection in the worst-case scenario.

The captive financing solution allows an employer in the middle-market segment to smooth out the volatility presented to the stop-loss carrier, thereby reducing risk by spreading the cost over a number of like-minded organizations who are committed to the same risk-management principles. In effect, this financing vehicle gives the middle-market employer the purchasing power of a 3,000-plus group.

How Does Captive Insurance Work?

A captive solution may be able to improve the efficiency of your health insurance financing. When you join a captive program, you and a number of other employers agree to share with other parties the risk for claims that are somewhat predictable and for claims that are somewhat unpredictable.

When you are in a captive program, a portion of your stop-loss premium is paid into a pool. If there are ten employers in the program, nobody knows who is going to have high-cost claimants—but group insurance actuarial models project it's likely to come from somewhere. When that expensive claim comes in, it is paid from the pool. The larger the pool, the more predictable the claim experience, and the more efficiently you and the other employers can purchase, independently and collectively.

For many employers, captive insurance presents a much more cost-effective way to manage risk than traditional stop-loss insurance approaches.

Advantages of captive financing:

1. **Reduction in cost due to greater purchasing power and efficiency—sustainability.** Insurance is the law of large numbers, and the captive financing model allows middle-market employers to share risk, smoothing out claim volatility and giving them the purchasing power of a 4,000- or 5,000-employee life group.

2. **Full decision-making control.** As a partially self-funded employer participating in a captive financing model, the plan is governed by ERISA and to a lesser extent the Affordable Care Act (ACA). ERISA-governed plans are flexible in nature and allow the employer more control over the plan design and financials. As the fiduciary of the plan assets, the employer will use a summary plan document, stop-loss contract, and third-party administrative agreement to govern the plan. Those documents serve as the employer's tools to control most decisions.

3. **Full access to all plan data.** The biggest benefit of being partially self-insured is that the plan sponsor (employer) owns the claim data rather than the insurer. This is particularly helpful when analyzing trends, which can be proactively addressed through insightful

financial reporting. Complete data transparency supports CDHP and a culture of well-being.

4. **Full transparency of all administrative and claims costs.** One of CDHP's core principles is transparency, and the partially self-insured captive financing model delivers it to the plan sponsor *and* the plan participants. All claims and administrative costs are disclosed to the plan sponsor, which gives the employer the ability to understand what is driving costs and, more importantly, how to improve that performance.

5. **Can create national scale and reach for middle-market employers.** Not all captive financing models are created to operate in multiple states across the country. However, the captive structure allows for the creation of a national solution because self-funded plans are governed by ERISA and permit the building of a national risk pool. That unique feature gives middle-market employers the opportunity to aggregate and leverage scale.

6. **Can create opportunities for like-minded organizations to strategically collaborate.** The principles that govern a captive financing model are critical to its long-term success. Sharing risk means sharing philosophy, and the captive structure promotes strategic collaboration among its member organizations. Through this collaboration, innovative and creative risk-management strategies can be developed to improve performance and the member experience.

Disadvantages of captive financing:

1. **Raising substantial capital is required if the organizations want to own the structure.** The captive financing model is expensive to construct due to the regulatory, actuarial, accounting, and legal work along with the appropriate level of financial reserves. Most estimates show it takes about $1 million to capitalize a captive and make it operational.

2. **Quality of service can be an issue depending on the program administrator.** To administer this financing model, employers can partner with a third-party administrator or work directly with the

health insurance carrier in an administrative services only capacity. Both types of strategic partners have access to provider networks on a local, regional, and national basis through their own proprietary network or through a leasing arrangement. Generally, TPAs offer more flexibility than ASO, and in both cases the quality of customer service can be negatively impacted.

3. **Limited tax benefits on the surplus created through the program.** One of the hidden values of the captive financing model is the tax-favorable nature of surplus in the captive layer. However, in recent years the tax laws have lessened the impact of this benefit in addition to higher regulatory scrutiny.

4. **Inability to spread risk if the pool of participating employers is too small.** Insurance is the law of large numbers, and the captive financing model allows for the strategic collaboration of multiple middle-market employers. However, the program must grow its membership to create scale and greater predictability of financial performance. If the risk pool isn't large enough or doesn't grow, financial sustainability of the program will be challenging.

5. **Additional management is required to run the program.** As discussed in the fully self-funded overview in this chapter, there are more moving parts to manage for this financial model to be effective versus the traditional fully insured financing model. And many of the moving parts present fiduciary liability for the plan sponsor (employer). As a result, the CFO/HR executive offices will be more involved in the administration of this model. A strong partnership between those two functions requires greater teamwork, and, depending on the organization, that can present challenges.

6. **Difficulty of entrance and exit compared to the open market.** When an employer partially self-insures, it is taking on all the risk of the employees' and their family members' claims and using reinsurance (stop-loss) to mitigate the financial impact of any one claimant or a collection of claimants. One of the advantages of this financing model is the transparency of all costs (both claims and administrative costs) for the plan sponsor. This informed insight is crucial for

the identification of trends and patterns. On the other hand, it also sets the expectation that the employer will share this information if and when it decides to evaluate returning to the fully insured market. If the plan sponsor's claims aren't running well, especially large claimants, obtaining a competitive quote could be challenging. Plan sponsors also need to make sure their plan documents, including the stop-loss contract, are structured in a way that they can exit the program with claims run-out protection (liability) when or if they leave. If those contract provisions aren't set up prudently, the plan sponsor's ability to exit without liability protection in place will make that transition financially unattractive.

Case Study: *Lincoln Academy*

For more than 200 years, Lincoln Academy has been serving the educational needs of secondary school students from the mid-coast of Maine. With an eye to managing expenses and keeping tuition costs reasonable, the school began investigating Captivated Health®. This evaluation came at a time when the school had already absorbed multiple double-digit renewals and was facing a 20% increase on its fully insured plan.

The initial Captivated Health® proposal came in at a 30% increase. Feeling that the bad claims year was behind them, Lincoln's CFO wanted to find a long-term solution that would provide control, stability, and savings. She opted for a whole new approach.

The school's first step was to gain access to its data. The Captivated Health® risk-management team worked with Lincoln Academy to analyze the information, and it devised strategies for mitigating the kinds of claims that were driving the year-over-year increases. The school determined that most of the adverse claim activity driving the large increases was being incurred by a small group of faculty and staff. The school's leadership decided it was the right time to move forward in joining Captivated Health®.

A critical component of the school's strategy was the decision to use the newly acquired data to provide full transparency to faculty and staff. This is a key feature of partially self-insured plans. It helps those covered under the plan to become aware of the actual cost of their care. As a result, they are better able to make informed and intelligent healthcare choices. Along with the decision to join Captivated Health ®, the school structured and implemented a multi-year health and well-being strategy. This strategy encompassed physical, financial, workplace, community, and mind/spirit components for faculty and staff.

What were the results of this strategy?

In the first year, the conservative assumptions recommended by the Captivated Health ® team, along with a favorable claims experience, allowed the plan to build up a significant reserve of $269,000. This reserve provided a hedge against future, unforeseen claims.

In the second year, the plan increased by only 6.4%—well below the double-digit increases it had been facing. As a result, the school was able to keep employee and staff contributions unchanged. During the same period, its reserves increased by $110,000. By its third year, the plan had achieved both predictability and stability.

The school was able to renew benefits without any faculty and staff contribution increases or watering-down of plan benefits.

Lincoln Academy's experience disproves the idea that an organization must be coming off a year with a very modest renewal rate increase in order to transition from a fully insured to a partially self-insured healthcare financing arrangement. Despite a challenging history of high claim activity, the school embraced Captivated Health ® as a solution. The secret to its success was full transparency to their faculty and a thoughtfully planned health and well-being program that resulted in significant financial improvements for the school and (just as important) in the overall health and well-being of its faculty and staff.

Conclusion

Our final message consists of two parts. First, we offer some practical advice to those organizational leaders considering adopting a CDHP and well-being strategy. Second, we close with some thoughts on the challenges facing the American healthcare system at the time this book went to press.

What Now?

Studies show that adopting a CDHP can lead to immediate savings in the first year of operation. It all starts with leadership and the belief that a shift to a CDHP and well-being strategy is the right approach for the company. The process begins with understanding this is an ongoing strategy, not a quick fix to check off a list. The decision to embrace and implement a CDHP is just the first step. Most successful strategies include:

1. a well-designed communication plan in advance of the rollout to prepare and educate employees on what a CDHP plan is and how it is different from the current plan,

2. meaningful (50% of deductible) employer contribution to the employees' HRA or HSA accounts,

3. benefit features that promote consumerism,

4. well-being strategies and incentives to engage employees, and

5. tracking and monitoring activities to determine what new tools can be introduced to help employees navigate their healthcare choices.

In addition to monitoring your plan's performance, it is important to survey your employees to gauge their satisfaction and understanding of their health plan and lifestyle choices. After the initial rollout of a CDHP, employees need to be creatively reminded of the value of a healthy lifestyle. There's no better way to foster enthusiasm and engagement than to demonstrate positive results with personal stories of success. Stories of personal weight loss, quitting smoking, joining a soccer league for physical activity, or participating in a simple walking campaign inspire. Success breeds success. Success can also motivate others when encouraged by peers. Newsletters, e-mail blasts, or office bulletins are an excellent way to deliver news and keep staff motivated, as are the online portals we've discussed in earlier chapters.

Engaging and supporting employees in a CDHP is a collaborative process involving organizational leaders and the HR team. Working closely with your employee benefits advisor and insurance company will allow you to maximize resources and share in the delivery of education in many ways.

CDHP is the cornerstone for achieving consumer engagement, and making the choice to adopt a CDHP and well-being strategy requires careful thought and consideration. Following the steps outlined in this book for a smooth transition will help you see positive results for your organization and its employees and dependents.

Health insurance is expensive because health care is expensive®.

Affordability can't be achieved without embracing healthcare cost and quality transparency and adopting innovative solutions like the CDHP to bend the healthcare trend.

The Road from Here

Before we close, permit us to share a few thoughts on the larger, and critical, issue of the American healthcare system and its current direction. The Affordable Care Act isn't working the way it was sold to the American people, and tens of millions of Americans are extremely dissatisfied with it. As a result, we believe more change is inevitable, regardless of the political winds prevailing at any given moment. The system as currently designed simply cannot sustain itself. It's not built on the right principles.

We embrace change and look forward to a new approach to healthcare reform in this country. We hope reform puts the focus where it belongs—on the consumer rather than the rulemakers. We believe such an approach must be grounded in the principles of affordability, accessibility, quality, innovation, and consumer empowerment through transparency and accountability.

Those five principles lie at the heart of any sustainable healthcare solution for this country.

Many people will tell you that such a solution is difficult or even impossible. We disagree. If we can fly a rocket from Cape Canaveral to Mars, land a Rover vehicle safely on the red planet, and use a remote control to drive that vehicle along a Martian surface 250 million miles away from the eastern coast of Florida, then we can solve the healthcare challenge in this country. We simply don't believe that our healthcare system is more complicated than that, and we hope you share the same belief and demand better.

Government, big hospital systems, big pharmaceutical companies, and big insurance companies (we call these groups by the collective name *rulemakers*) created our current healthcare system, and they use a complex, opaque process called coding and billing to administer it. It's the system all four of those groups created, and it's completely and purposefully opaque to hide the real driver behind rising health insurance premiums—rising healthcare costs. It's opaque because that's how people in those four entities like to work. Given the choice, they prefer to work in a world where consumers don't get clear answers to fair questions about quality, cost, and overall value so they can behave rationally just like in every other consumer decision in their lives.

You can't possibly improve what you can't measure, and you can't possibly measure what you can't see. We will never fix the rising cost of health care if the rulemakers who are devoted to opacity are given the job of designing the reform package. It would be like asking the fox to guard the henhouse, only to return and find all the hens are missing! Whether we like it or not, big government, big hospital systems, big pharmaceutical companies, and big insurance companies are the collective fox. The healthcare consumers are the collective hens. This state of affairs needs to change, and it doesn't start with government insisting it can do better by taking it over. If we think health care is expensive now, wait until it's "free."

We wrote this book to advocate on behalf of CDHPs as an under-examined solution for today's healthcare challenges. We passionately believe CDHPs save both healthcare consumers and employers money (proven fact) and support the consumer's rights and responsibilities in health care. We don't believe "We can't tell you that" is an acceptable answer when a consumer asks about the quality, cost, and value of their health care. If you're willing and passionate, as we are, to put the power of a whole nation of informed health-care consumers behind the effort to reform our broken healthcare system in the United States, then please share this book and its insights with others. You, the reader, are in a position to change the system for the better—one engaged, educated, and empowered consumer at a time.

Glossary

Claim: Notification to an insurance company requesting payment of the amount due under the terms of the policy for whatever incidence has occurred.

Co-pay: The amount of money (or percentage of charges) for basic or supplemental health services that an employee is required to pay, as set forth in his or her health plan. A visit to the doctor's office or the emergency room can generate a co-pay.

COBRA (Consolidated Omnibus Budget Reconciliation Act): This law requires an employer to allow an employee to remain temporarily covered under the employer's group health plan after the loss of a job. The beneficiary may have to pay both his or her share plus the employer's share of the premium.

Consumer-driven health plan (CDHP): A broad definition incorporating several emerging healthcare strategies that heighten consumer awareness. Through various plan incentives, a CDHP lays out the cost and utilization of healthcare services. It describes numerous mechanisms for providing health insurance or funding healthcare costs, all of which encourage individuals to become actively involved in making their own decisions regarding their health.

Deductible: The minimum amount the employee must pay before the insurance company will begin to make payments (above and beyond the deductible) for covered medical services. Plans may have both per-individual and per-family deductibles.

Deductible leveraging: The practice of increasing the deductible each year to counterbalance overall healthcare inflation.

Employee benefits consultant: A consultant knowledgeable in the areas of comprehensive benefit plans. An employee benefits consultant uses his or her expertise, along with a firm comprehension of the company's work environment, business goals, and benefit objectives to achieve the employer's business objectives.

Encouragement-based health and wellness program: A program in which no rewards, incentives, or penalties are offered in connection with the wellness program, or any reward, incentive, or penalty offered is dependent solely on participation in the wellness activities, and the results obtained by those activities do not affect the outcome. Encouragement-based programs aren't subject to any special rules, providing they're equally available to all similarly situated individuals.

Explanation of benefits (EOB): A statement from the insurer about an employee's health claim. The statement should include information about the provider, the date of service, the service itself, how much the provider charges for this service, how much the insurer considers to be a reasonable price for this service, and the amount the insurer paid the healthcare provider. It may also include information on how much you, as the patient, may be responsible for paying.

Federal Insurance Contributions Act (FICA) tax: A federal payroll tax imposed on both employees and employers to fund Social Security and Medicare.

First-dollar coverage: A health insurance plan that typically begins to pay its share of the employee's covered services beginning with the first service they receive within the plan network. In a fee-for-service plan, payments for covered services begin after you've met the deductible.

Flexible spending account (FSA): A benefit account (under Section 125 of the Internal Revenue Code) that offers employees a choice between permissible taxable benefits, including cash, and nontaxable benefits, such as life and health insurance, vacations, retirement plans, and childcare. Though a common core of benefits may be required, the employee is allowed to determine how his or her remaining benefit dollars are to be allocated, choosing each type of benefit from the total dollar amount promised by the employer.

Healthcare trend: The healthcare industry's term for medical cost inflation. Healthcare trend consists primarily of two components: unit cost (the actual cost of each health service or product) and utilization (the number of times health services or products are accessed).

Health maintenance organization (HMO): A healthcare system that assumes both the financial risks associated with providing comprehensive medical services (insurance and service risk) and the responsibility for healthcare delivery in a particular geographic area to its members, usually in return for a fixed, prepaid fee. Financial risk may be shared with the providers participating in the HMO.

Health reimbursement arrangement (HRA): An IRS-sanctioned program that allows an employer to reimburse medical expenses paid by participating employees, thus yielding a tax advantage to offset healthcare costs.

Health savings account (HSA): A tax-advantaged medical savings account available to employees enrolled in an HDHP. The funds contributed to the account aren't subject to federal income tax at the time of the deposit. Unlike with an FSA, funds roll over and accumulate year over year if not spent. HSAs are owned by the individual, which differentiates them from the company-owned HRA. Funds may be used to pay for qualified medical expenses at any time without federal tax liability.

High-deductible health plan (HDHP): A health insurance plan with lower premiums and higher deductibles than a traditional health plan. Participating in a qualified HDHP is a requirement for HSAs and other tax-advantaged programs.

Managed-care plan: A plan that provides comprehensive health services to members and offers financial incentives for patients to use the providers who belong to the plan. Examples of managed-care plans include HMOs, PPOs, exclusive provider organizations (EPOs), and point of service plans (POSs).

Out-of-pocket costs: Healthcare costs that aren't covered by the health insurance plan and are paid by the employee.

Performance-based health and wellness program: A program that uses rewards, incentives, or penalties tied to an individual's ability to meet a certain performance standard related to a specific health factor, such as reaching a healthy body weight or body mass index (BMI), lowering cholesterol, or quitting smoking. Individuals with medical conditions that make it impossible or medically inadvisable to reach such performance standards must be provided alternative standards.

Preferred provider organization (PPO): A healthcare organization composed of physicians, hospitals, or other providers that provide healthcare services at a reduced fee. A PPO is similar to an HMO, but care is paid for as it's received (fee-per-service) instead of in advance in the form of a scheduled fee. PPOs may also offer more flexibility by allowing for visits to out-of-network services.

Premium: An agreed-upon fee (lump sum) paid for coverage of medical benefits for a defined benefit period. Premiums can be paid by employers, unions, or employees, or shared by both the insured individual and the plan sponsor.

Preventive care: A healthcare program designed to prevent and reduce illnesses by providing such services as physical examinations. This care is in opposition to curative care, which goes into effect only after an illness has been determined.

Qualified high-deductible health plan (QHDHP): QHDHP is part of the Medicare Modernization Act signed into law in 2003. Its purpose is to lower healthcare costs by encouraging plan members to analyze their healthcare decisions, while making insurance premiums more affordable to everyone. An HSA or HRA would be used with the HDHP to help pay for the deductible costs. See *high-deductible health plan (HDHP)*.

Third-party administrator (TPA): A third-party administrator is the same as an administrative services only company. The duties of the TPA is to serve as the liaison between the insured person or company and the health insurance provider. Typically, the TPA will file claims for the insured, but will also certify insurability for the insurance company.

Unit cost: The actual cost of each health service or product accessed by employees, such as visits to health services providers, filled prescriptions, or medical equipment. Unit cost is, along with utilization, one of two components of healthcare trend, the industry's term for medical cost inflation.

Utilization: The number of times a medical service is accessed or a product is purchased. Also called units of service, utilization is, along with unit cost, one of two components of healthcare trend, the industry's term for medical cost inflation.

Well-being program: A program dedicated to the transformation of an organization's entire culture toward a mind-set of continuous improvement and personal accountability, including, but not limited to, all aspects of individual health.

Wellness Council of America (WELCOA): An organization dedicated to the promotion of worksite wellness.

Endnotes

[1] PBS NewsHour, July 13, 2016.

[2] Kaiser Health News, July 13, 2016.

[3] Milliman Medical Index.

[4] Kaiser Health Benefits, SHRM.

[5] Ibid.

[6] National Health Statistics report.

[7] http://www.devenir.com/research/2016-year-end-devenir-hsa-research-report/

[8] U.S. Department of Labor, Field Assistance Bulletin No. 2008-02.

Index

For more information on Mark S. Gaunya and/or Jennifer A. Borislow, email info@strategicvisionpublishing.com